The Ultimate Beginner Guitar Method Book For Hobby Players

Written by Michael Gumley
Copyright © 2024 Michael Gumley

All rights reserved. No part of this book may be reproduced in any form or by any electronic or mechanical means, including information storage and retrieval systems, without permission in writing from the author.

Editing by Michael Gumley
Front cover image by Michael Gumley
Book layout & design by Michael Gumley

All musical examples were written and/or arranged by the author with the exception of the guitar riffs which are provided here for educational purposes under the *Fair Use Act*. All rights belong to the copyright owner.

Printed and bound in Australia by GVP Education
First Edition printed in January 2024
This Edition printed in January 2024
Published by GVP Education Pty Ltd
80 Raleigh St, Essendon, Vic, Australia, 3040

Warning!

Unauthorised Photocopying, Recreation, or Distribution is Prohibited

© Melbourne Guitar Academy
Adult Guitar Method Book
www.MelbourneGuitarAcademy.com

Contents

Introduction 1

Key Concepts 8

Getting Into Guitar 11

Study Pieces 29

Riffs 45

Fretboard Knowledge 49

The Level Up System 55

Chord & Strumming 62

Practice Log 70

© Melbourne Guitar Academy
Adult Guitar Method Book
www.MelbourneGuitarAcademy.com

Welcome To The Adult Beginner Guitar Method Book

Congratulations on your decision to work through this beginner guitar method book!

Every single beginner method I've come across in almost two decades of teaching has been written to help the student become a professional jazz or classical musician. As a result, the contents are overly complex, academic in their approach and out of touch with the needs of people learning the guitar as a hobby.

Most of these beginner guitar books start with single-note playing and have a big emphasis on reading standard music notation while skipping several important elements of contemporary guitar playing altogether.

By 2016, I was so fed up with not having a beginner guitar method book that covered everything I needed it to that I decided to write my own.

As soon as I switched to using my books in lessons my students loved it. Not only did they learn faster because we skipped reading music and got straight into playing, but they also got to start playing the songs they liked which made the whole learning experience so much more fun and engaging.

I quickly became the top teacher at my local music school and earned a reputation as the go-to guitar teacher in my local area.

After a few years, I wanted to make the books even better and came up with the idea of a level-up system. This resulted in me creating my Guitar Ninjas Curriculum which is now used in over 20 studios all around the world.

While kids loved the Guitar Ninjas books, some of my adults found the karate-style gimmick a little childish and wanted something a little more mature.

I also realised that not everyone wanted to spend 8-10 years getting to Black Belt level, especially when most radio-level songs become playable by level 4 which only takes 2-3 years.

The bottom line is that most folks just want to sit in their bedroom or around a campfire with a few friends and enjoy playing their favourite songs without having to commit hours each week to practice.

With this in mind, I decided to create a beginner guitar method that's perfect for casual players. If you're like most people, you're in it for fun, not to become a guitar superstar.

This method is for you!

Welcome To The Adult Beginner Guitar Method Book

Our brand new Adult Beginner Guitar Method has been reduced to include only the absolute essentials of what you need to get started with playing guitar.

We've kept the fast learning and gamification from Guitar Ninjas that people love while ditching the ninja gimmick which made a lot of adult students feel childish.

We've also retained the *Rapid Results* training which is a key feature of lessons at Melbourne Guitar Academy, this means you'll still make great progress and feel good about your guitar playing even if you can only commit to a few 10-minute practice sessions each week.

Get ready for a simple, step-by-step guide to all the basics, complete with fun worksheets to track your progress and keep the learning process exciting.

Oh, and there's a new Level-Up system too. It lets you play along with any song, even if you're brand new to guitar.

I started playing around with this idea when I first wrote the Guitar Ninja series, and after a few years of tweaking, we're doubling down on what works and ditching what doesn't!

Now, you can jam to thousands of songs right from day one. It's not the usual way, but that's why it's so awesome!

So, thanks for picking up your copy of **The Ultimate Beginner Guitar Method For Adult Hobby Players**. I can't wait to help you become an awesome guitar player, no matter your ambition or what level of success you're aiming for.

Get excited! Your guitar journey is about to begin!

Why People Fail At Guitar

Let's be real with each other for a second.

Learning the guitar isn't inherently tough.

So why do many people struggle with it?

It's not because the guitar is physically demanding or because the concepts are overly complex. It all boils down to one thing: the guitar, like any other instrument, doesn't provide instant gratification.

Becoming skilled at playing the guitar is simple. You just need to stick with lessons and keep practicing until you're good. It's that straightforward.

But here's the catch: We humans tend to opt for the path of least resistance and avoid anything that resembles hard work...

While you might be excited about learning guitar now, when you encounter obstacles and your initial enthusiasm wanes, you might lose motivation to practice. You might even convince yourself that you never really wanted to learn guitar in the first place.

Our modern world, filled with video games, social media, smartphones, and other instant gratifications, hasn't helped. Learning guitar, in contrast, demands time and repetition to turn short-term knowledge into long-term muscle memory.

It's like getting in great shape. Everyone knows you need to eat well and exercise consistently to achieve it. The theory is simple, but committing to a diet and exercise routine over an extended period is the challenging part.

This is where we come in.

Just as a personal trainer can create a program and keep you on track, our Beginner Guitar Method is your program, and we are your trainers. We're here to guide you on your guitar journey and help you stick with it, even when the going gets tough.

So as long as you acknowledge that learning the guitar is going to take a few years and that you're prepared to commit (even when times get tough) you'll eventually get good!

How This Book Works

This book is split into two parts:

The first part called the **Fundamentals Section**, covers all the essential skills, concepts, and techniques you need to play the guitar. It includes practice pieces to help you master basic skills and explanations of important topics for beginner guitarists. You'll also find drill worksheets that focus on honing specific skills over several practice sessions, much like how a personal trainer uses a workout planner to track progress over time.

Our goal is to help you see improvement over time, rather than constantly searching for new exercises each week.

The second part of the book introduces the **Level-Up System** designed to help you learn songs and build a repertoire of pieces you can play. We've made it so clear and simple that you can play along with any chord-based song right from the start, even if you're a complete beginner. We're confident that you'll succeed within the framework we provide.

It's worth noting that this book doesn't follow a strict linear path. Instead, you'll work through both sections simultaneously.

The accompanying online course will provide a structured practice plan. Your teacher may also offer recommendations on what to learn in which order.

Plan to spend 8 to 12 weeks going through all the content, but feel free to go at your own pace—faster or slower. Just be sure to complete each lesson and regularly review the material.

Remember, mastery comes from repetition. It's more effective to deeply understand a few concepts than to learn many things at a surface level.

Using The Checklists & Worksheets

This book is meant to be interactive. Keep a pencil or pen handy at all times, and be ready to write, draw, and check-off items as you complete them.

As a teacher, one of my biggest frustrations is when students play something once and think they're done...

Learning guitar isn't a race you complete once. It's more like a gym workout where you aim for a certain number of repetitions or do an exercise for a specific duration. Having said this, we do know that doing the same thing repeatedly can get dull.

To keep things fresh and engaging, I've designed various challenges. These challenges involve repeating the same physical movements over and over but presenting them in new ways to keep practising them fresh and interesting.

Essentially, when you start to feel bored, we introduce a new way of doing the exercise or a new objective to renew your focus.

I've also created structured learning methods that consist of 3 to 5 steps. These methods usually form the basis of the challenges. By completing each challenge and checking off the boxes, you not only get the satisfaction of immediate accomplishment, but you also reinforce your long-term skill development.

Here's a tip: Don't think that once something is checked off, it's finished forever. I recommend repeating the same challenges several times and using different coloured pens or pencils to keep track of them.

Alternatively, you can download new worksheets from the online course and complete them as many times as you like.

Many lessons and pages include tick boxes to help you keep track of different challenges and see exactly where you are at and what's coming up next. This way, you can stay organized and on top of your learning journey.

"Practice isn't something you did, it's something you do" - Brad Lea

Setting Your Expectations For Success

When it comes to learning the guitar, you'll start with a lot of enthusiasm and be on a high for the first couple of weeks. For many guitarists, somewhere between weeks three and twelve, you might hit your first obstacle and feel frustrated. Frustration often arises when your expectations don't match your progress.

People sometimes say that having low expectations leads to a happy life, but I disagree. I do believe in having high expectations for yourself and what you can achieve. However, many underestimate the time and effort required to learn the guitar and are unrealistic about how long it takes to learn.

It's crucial to be realistic about the time frame. Don't compare yourself to professional guitar players with years of experience. If you dedicate three 30-minute practice sessions each week, in 12 to 18 months, you'll likely be able to play along confidently with most of your favorite radio-level songs.

More frequent practice leads to faster improvement, while less practice means slower progress.

If you don't practice at all between lessons, your progress will be very slow, but over time, you can still accumulate enough skill to become good, even though it might take years.

So just because you're making slower progress than you anticipated, it doesn't mean you should chuck in the towel.

Your success on the guitar depends on what you do during the hours we're not together, the expectations you set for yourself, and your commitment to them.

Learning the guitar will be challenging at times. It might take a few months or even a couple of years to get really good, depending on your goals. But as long as you don't stop taking lessons and don't quit playing altogether, you'll eventually accumulate the skills and knowledge to play at the level you desire.

Take solace knowing that at some point, even your favourite guitar player wasn't that good at guitar. They never gave up and became the world-class guitarist they are today. As long as you don't quit, you'll eventually reach a level where you can play their stuff.

Now, if someone like Jimi Hendrix practised for five hours a day for over a decade before he became famous, it's essential to set realistic expectations about how long it's going to take you to get to the same level of skill with your guitar playing.

Setting Your Expectations For Success

Don't quit after three months because you're not at the level Jimi Hendrix was ten years into his guitar-playing journey. It's just not a fair comparison.

Instead, put yourself on a trajectory based on what you can commit to your guitar practice and set your expectations according to the time, effort, and energy that your schedule and life circumstances allow.

Having said all that, the good news is that I can help you achieve fast results by setting a clear path for you to follow, helping you focus on the essentials, and providing methods of accelerated learning so that what would normally take someone a decade, will take you considerably less time!

What took Jimi Hendrix 10 years to figure out we can probably get you to in 3 to 5 years by working smarter, not just harder. He already did the hard work of figuring things out, and we have the benefit of looking at what he did and following the path he already created.

We can also use the **Level-Up System** to play along with most songs in a simplified way, so you don't have to wait 3 years before you get to attempt playing any of his songs.

While they won't sound exactly like the original recordings, they'll be recognizable to anyone listening. As you progress, we can revisit these songs and bring them closer to the original over time. This approach allows you to enjoy playing your favourite songs right away rather than waiting until you're "*good enough*" to start working on them.

Just like everyone has the potential to have visible six-pack abs or a great body. Everyone has the potential to become a great guitar player.

It just comes down to whether you're willing to put in what is required consistently over a long enough period to achieve a high level of skill.

It's simply a mental game of committing long enough to achieve the desired outcome...

Do you have what it takes?

Let's find out!

Key Concept 1: The Success Formula For Guitar

To become a good guitar player, you only need to do three things:

1) Attend your weekly lessons
2) Practice regularly at home
3) Never give up!

By following these three steps, you have a 100% guarantee of becoming a skilled guitar player. Stay committed and let time work its magic!

Remember, practice makes progress!

"It takes time to be a success, but time is all it takes"

Key Concept 2: The Ladder

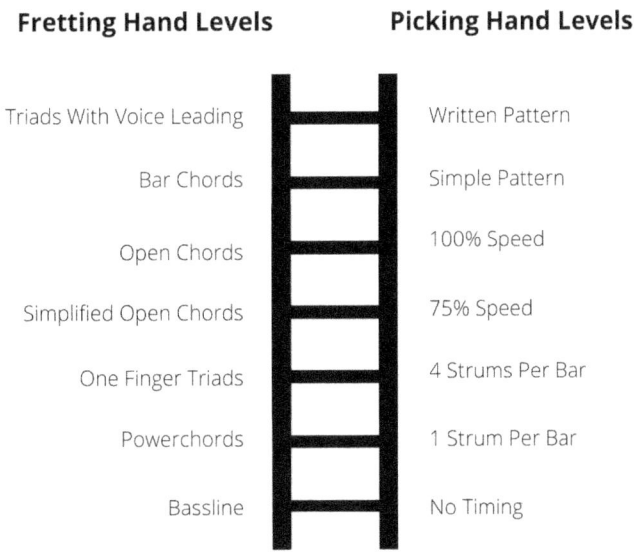

I firmly believe that the traditional way of learning guitar is completely backwards, which is why many beginners struggle when they first start learning.

Think about going to the gym and trying to do a 100kg (220lb) bench press on your very first day working out. For 99.9% of people, it's likely to end in failure.

Unfortunately, many guitar teachers make a similar mistake by introducing Open Chords early in their lessons. These chords can be quite challenging, especially for beginners and young learners with small hands who are still developing their fine motor skills.

Most teachers and authors are completely unaware of the concept of **Levelling and Layering** where any skill or technique can be broken down into simpler steps. These steps lay the groundwork for what we eventually consider *standard chords* on guitar.

Instead of setting ourselves up for failure by attempting to play something beyond our physical capabilities, we break things down into smaller more achievable levels or *next steps* to work on. This approach ensures that you can learn and succeed at a level appropriate for you, resulting in a feeling of accomplishment and confidence at each level.

The ladder above illustrates levels for both the picking and fretting hands, highlighting that there are numerous levels preceding the introduction of *Open Chords* and *Bar Chords*, which is where most students traditionally start.

By following this ladder approach, you can build a solid foundation of skill and a repertoire of songs while gradually increasing the intensity as your skill level allows. This will make for a much more enjoyable journey.

Key Concept 3: The Chain Method

We've got a special motto: "**Say it three times and play it three times**."

It's a fantastic way to learn music fast and remember notes quickly. But we've taken it a step further with what we call the **Chain Method**.

Here's how the Chain Method works:

1. Say the first chunk of music three times, then play it three times.
2. Say the second chunk of music three times, then play it three times.
3. Combine the first and second chunks into a bigger chunk, say it, and play it three times.
4. Now, let's learn the third chunk of music by saying it and playing it three times.
5. Then, learn the fourth chunk of music in the same way—say it and play it three times.
6. Combine the third and fourth chunks into a bigger chunk, say it, and play it three times.
7. Finally, put all four chunks together and say and play the entire line of music three times.

If the piece is longer than just one line, no worries. We simply repeat this process with the new line of music, building the entire example piece by piece, just like you would forge together links in a chain.

Using the **Chain Method** might feel like it takes longer, but allows you to memorise music and develop the muscle memory required to play the guitar far more quickly than mindless repetition or playing the piece from start to finish over and over.

Section 1

Getting Into Guitar

In this chapter, you will be learning all of the fundamental skills and concepts you need to play guitar.

Tuning The Guitar

Having your guitar in tune will be very important whether you play on your own or with other people.

To tune a guitar all you need to do is pick the string and then turn the tuning peg that matches that string.

Now in order for the guitar to be in tune, each string has to match a particular pitch.

I like to say the phrase **E**aster **B**unnies **G**o **D**ancing **A**t **E**aster.

The first letter of each word becomes the name of the string, and the note we need to tune to.

- The first string is tuned to an E note (thinnest string)
- The second string is tuned to a B note
- The third string is tuned to an G note
- The fourth string is tuned to a D note
- The fifth string is tuned to an A note
- The sixth string is also tuned to an E note. (thickest string)

Most tuners these days will simply give you the name of the string you are playing and tell you whether you are sharp (#) or flat (♭).

If you are really out of tune, you may need to give the string a big twist in order to put it back into the right range for the tuner to pick up.

EG. If you are tuning the E string but your tuner is showing you a B note, you need to tighten the string so it goes from B to C to D and then to E.

Tip: Watch the video on *How To Tune Your Guitar* to see how tuning works.

How To Pick

Today, we're going to learn a very important skill: how to pick the strings on your guitar!

To do this, you'll need a special tool called a **guitar pick** or **plectrum**. It's a small, teardrop-shaped piece of plastic that helps you make a sound on the guitar. If you don't have a guitar pick, you can also use the bottom edge of your thumb.

How To Pick

1. Hold the guitar pick between your thumb and first finger, (see the image below)
2. Point the pick back towards the guitar.
3. Bring the pick to the first string, right over the middle of the sound hole.
4. Pluck the string with a small, quick, downward motion from your wrist (not your elbow)
5. Let the string ring out for a few seconds, so you can hear the sound it makes.
6. Now, let's repeat this 10 times on the first string, which is the thinnest string.
7. Repeat the same motion 10 times on each of the 6 strings.

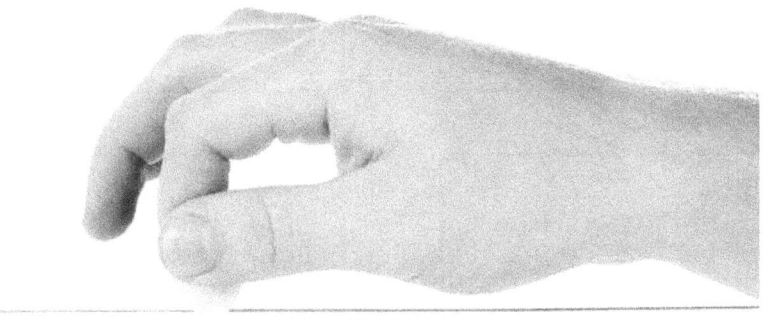

Tip: Remember, when you're picking, make sure to grip the pick firmly in the middle and use the same amount of movement as if you were moving a computer mouse about 2cm on the screen.

Picking Drills

These simple exercises are great for building picking hand coordination.

You'll notice boxes with the letters D, U and A or E within them.

D = Down Picks (downstrokes)
U = Up Picks (upstrokes)
A = Alternate Picking (where you alternate between down and up strokes with each pick)
E = Efficiency Picking (where you use the most efficient combination of down and up strokes)

Play each example 10 times in-a-row without a mistake to earn the tick.

#	Exercise	Picking
1	10 Picks On Each String	D U A
2	1 & 2	D U A
3	1 & 3	D U A
4	1 & 6	D U A
5	1 2 3	D U E
6	3 2 1	D U E
7	1 3 2 3	D U A
8	4 3 2 1	D U E
9	6 3 2 1	D U E
10	6 3 2 1 2 3	D U E
11	1-2, 1-3, 1-4, 1-5, 1-6	D U A
12	6-5, 6-4, 6-3, 6-2, 6-1	D U A

Speed Tracker

BPM	Ex 1	Ex 2	Ex 3	Ex 4	Ex 5	Ex 6	Ex 7	Ex 8	Ex 9	Ex 10	Ex 11	Ex 12
60												
80												
100												
120												

How To Fret Notes

In this lesson you will learn the second fundamental skill: How to fret notes.

A fret is a small metal bar embedded within the neck of the guitar. Putting your finger down behind a fret and squeezing shortens the length of the string and changes the pitch that you hear. Think of each fret on the guitar like a key on a piano. The lower the fret, the lower the note, the higher the fret the higher the note.

How To Fret Notes

1. Hold your fretting hand as if you had an imaginary can of drink in it.
2. Rotate your hand so your thumb is pointing up towards the roof.
3. Place your thumb in the middle of the neck (where the spine would be)
4. Curve your finger and bring the tip down right up near the edge of the first fret of the first string.
5. Squeeze hard enough to make the string press against the wood underneath.
6. Pluck the string with your picking hand and let it ring out for several seconds. (don't let go until you're ready to move)
7. Now move to the 2nd fret and pick it, then the 3rd fret etc.
8. Play all the way to Fret 12 and back again!

Ex 1. How to fret - close to the fret

Ex 2. How not to fret - in the middle of two frets

Tip: Be as close to the fret as you can get without actually touching it. Don't press on top of the fret, and don't be in the middle between two frets.

Finger Coordination Drills

These simple exercises are great for fretting hand coordination and dexterity. Aim to complete at least one exercise per practice session to accelerate the rate at which you develop your fretting skills.

Assign 1 Finger per fret and focus on smoothly transitioning from note to note.

Challenges 1 = 1 String - 2 = 2 Strings - 6 = 6 Strings - Z = Zig-Zag

Play each example 10 times in a row without a mistake to earn the tick.

You can use the table at the bottom of this page to measure your speed over time.

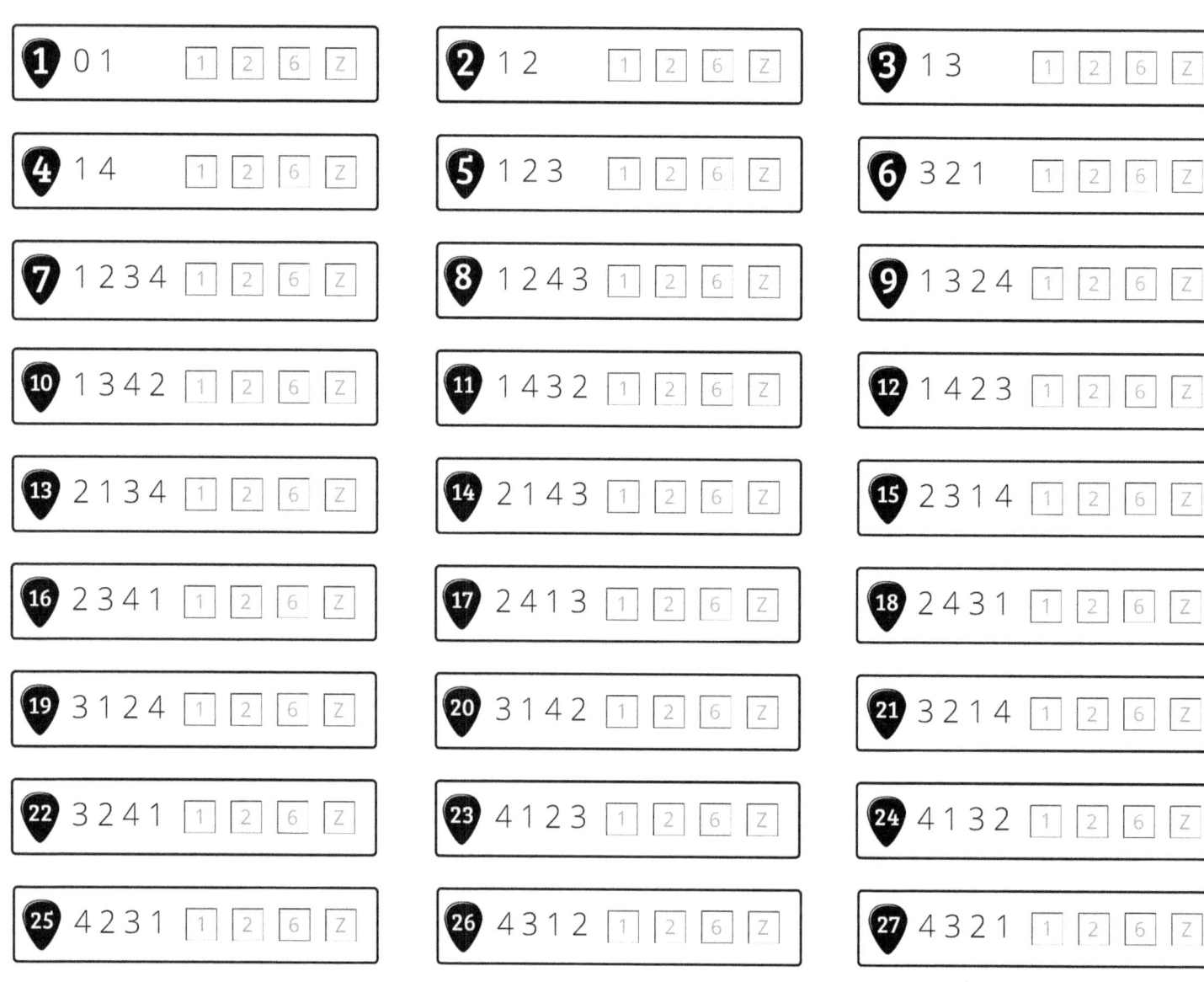

1. 0 1	2. 1 2	3. 1 3
4. 1 4	5. 1 2 3	6. 3 2 1
7. 1 2 3 4	8. 1 2 4 3	9. 1 3 2 4
10. 1 3 4 2	11. 1 4 3 2	12. 1 4 2 3
13. 2 1 3 4	14. 2 1 4 3	15. 2 3 1 4
16. 2 3 4 1	17. 2 4 1 3	18. 2 4 3 1
19. 3 1 2 4	20. 3 1 4 2	21. 3 2 1 4
22. 3 2 4 1	23. 4 1 2 3	24. 4 1 3 2
25. 4 2 3 1	26. 4 3 1 2	27. 4 3 2 1

Speed Tracker

BPM	Ex 1	Ex 2	Ex 3	Ex 4	Ex 5	Ex 6	Ex 7	Ex 8	Ex 9	Ex 10	Ex _	Ex _	Ex _	Ex _	Ex _	Ex _	Ex _
60																	
80																	
100																	
120																	

Reading Guitar Music

In this lesson you will learn how to read guitar music.

As guitarists, we are lucky to have our own system of music notation called **Guitar Tablature** (or TAB for short). Guitar Tablature is a system of lines and numbers that correspond to our strings and the frets we need to play. Although reading standard music notation is a very important skill, as beginners we want to start playing and having fun RIGHT NOW! We can come back and learn to read music once we already know how to play.

Understanding Tablature

First, you need to visualize the fretboard as if the guitar was laid out on a table in front of you with the thinest string on top and the thickest string on the bottom

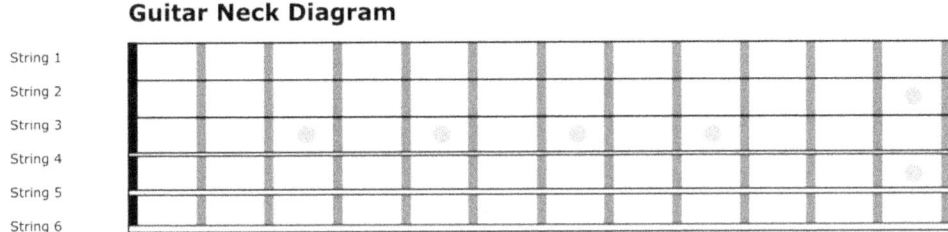

Secondly, you need to reduce the diagram to only include the 6 horizontal lines which represent the strings. Remember: Thin on top, thick on bottom.

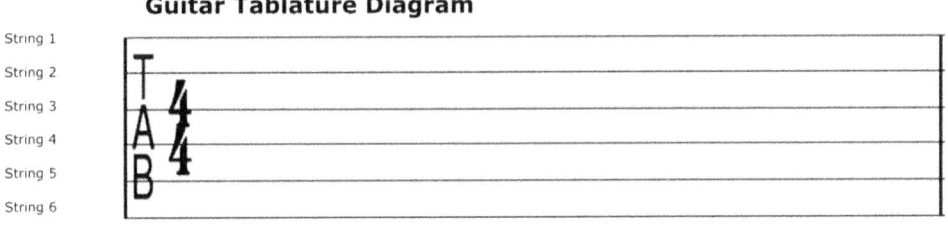

Try to first read, and then play the following examples:

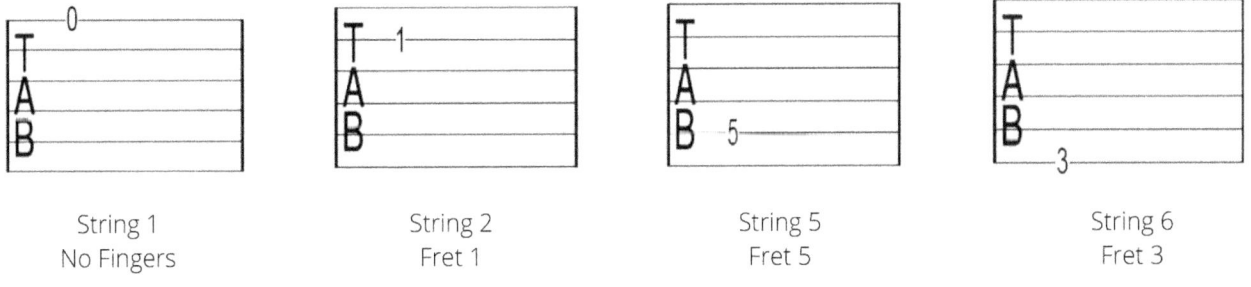

17

© Melbourne Guitar Academy
Adult Guitar Method Book
www.MelbourneGuitarAcademy.com

Reading Drills

The guitar is one of the easiest instruments to learn because we can use numbers to tell us which frets to play instead of learning how to read standard musical notation.

When it comes to reading Guitar Music (known formally as *Tablature* or "*Tab*" for short) you need to remember two things:

- The number is the fret you need to put your finger on.
- The line the number is found on represents the string you need to play.

Use the examples below to help you practice reading Guitar Tab. First, you read the fret number and say it aloud, Second, play it on your guitar. **S = Say it, P = Play It**

Notes On String 1 (thinnest string)

```
T |--0----7----3----12---8----10---2----4----1----11--|| S
A |                                                   ||
B |4/4                                                || P
```

Notes On String 2

```
T |--12---5----8----3----0----1----10---7----11---2---|| S
A |                                                   ||
B |                                                   || P
```

Notes On String 3

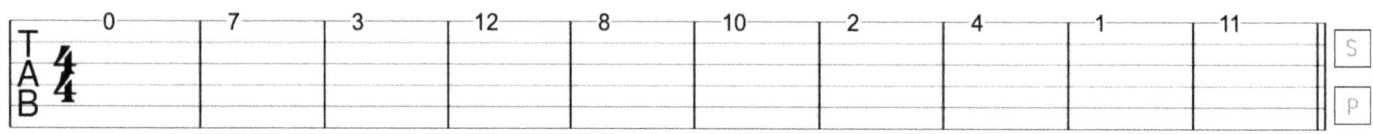

Notes On String 4

```
T |                                                   || S
A |--12---9----11---8----10---6----0----3----1----4---||
B |                                                   || P
```

Notes On String 5

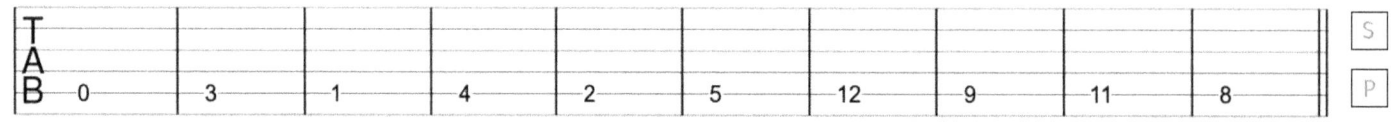

Notes On String 6

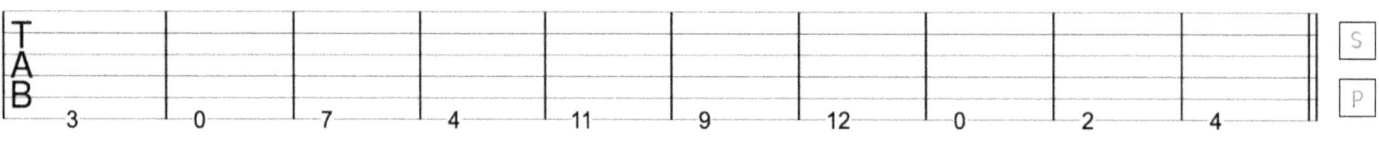

18

© Melbourne Guitar Academy
www.MelbourneGuitarAcademy.com

Reading Drills

Here are some additional reading drills to help you develop your ability to read guitar tabs quickly.

Remember: The number is the fret, and the line is the string.

Notes On String 1 & 2

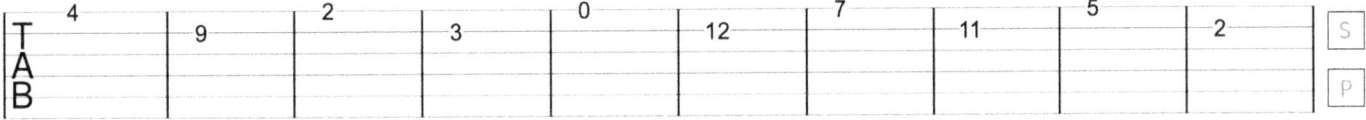

Notes On Strings 1-3

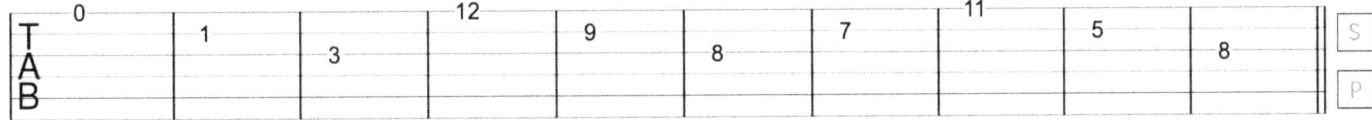

Notes On String 4-6

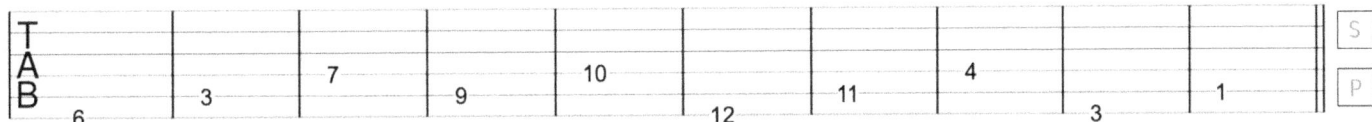

Notes On String 2-5

T	1				5			3			S
A		4		8			12		6		
B			11			7				0	P

Notes On All 6 Strings

T					1					S
A			7	8		12	10		6	
B		5						4		P
	0							3		

Notes On All 6 Strings

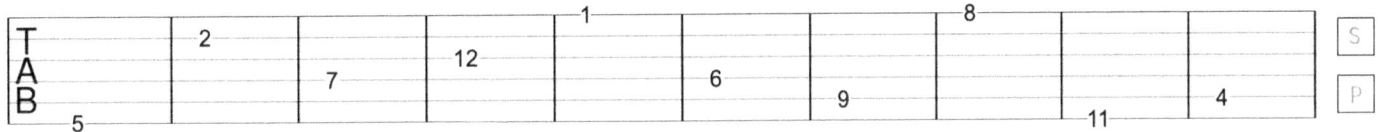

If you're looking for an additional challenge you can try to figure out which note is found at the frets in each example above.

Learning not just the tabs but the location of the notes is very important and will make reading actual music much easier when we cover it later on.

Notes Along The First String

In this lesson, you will learn the notes along the first string and use both picking and fretting together in order to play them.

The first example below is the *E Natural Minor Scale*. We've got a special process to help you learn it quickly and effectivly!

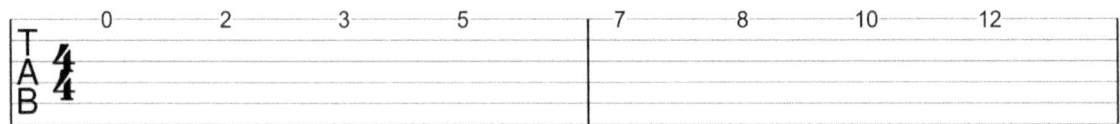

1. Say the first four numbers out loud three times.
2. Play the first four number three times.
3. Say the second four numbers out loud three times.
4. Play the second four number three times.
5. Say all eight numbers out loud three times.
6. Play all eight numbers three times

We call this the **Say It Three Times, Play It Three Times** method. We have found that it is the best way to help you learn and memorise new information and to help you retain it long term. In the case of longer pieces of music you should do each indiviudal line of music three times each before putting the entire piece together.

Once you have learned a piece of music we recommend you try to play it in new ways to reinforce what you know and keep practice fun and exciting with some additional challenges. Try some of the following:

- Playing it backwards (from 12 to 0).
- Playing it using only upstrokes.
- Playing it while standing up.
- Playing it with your eyes shut.
- Playing it 10 times in-a-row without any mistakes.

How many of the challenges above can you do?

Strumming

In this lesson, we will revisit the *E Natural Minor Scale we* learned previously while also integrating it with a new technique called **Strumming**.

Strumming is when you play two or more strings at the same time using one single motion. Use the same motion as if you had just washed your hands and were flicking the water off.

We can identify strumming in Guitar Tab when the numbers are stacked up on top of each other like the examples below:

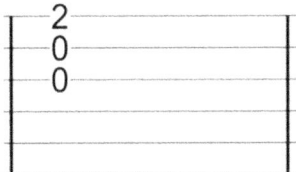

In the first example you can see three 0's stacked up on top of each other, this means they need to be played at the same time using the strum technique. In the second example we are fretting the 2nd fret of string 1 but still strumming the 2nd and 3rd string openly. Try playing the example below:

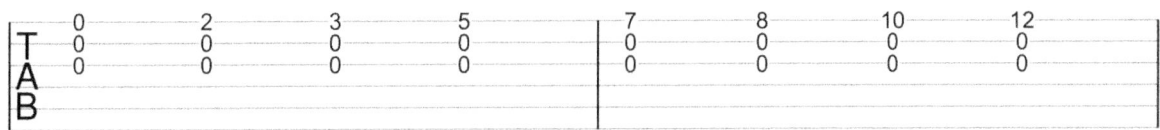

Hopefully you noticed that it was the same E Natural Minor Scale you learned in the previous lesson, but this time you are using strumming to include other strings. You should still:

- Play it forward three times.
- Play it backward three times.
- Play it while standing up.
- Play it with your eyes shut.
- Play it 10 times in a row without any mistakes.

Picking Patterns

In this lesson you will you will learn how to combine your E Natural Minor scale with picking patterns to create beautiful sounds on the guitar.

A **Picking Pattern** is a sequential pattern of strings that we pick which is repeated across several bars of music (or even an entire piece of music). Below is an example of what a picking pattern looks like in Guitar Tab:

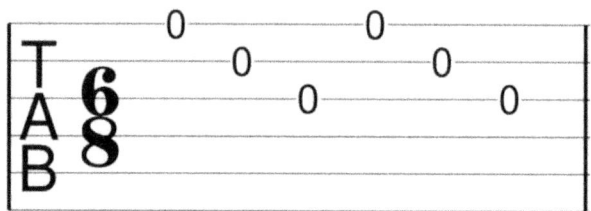

In the example above we are still playing across multiple strings, but unlike strumming where the numbers are stacked upon each other and played at the same time, we are going to play each note individually. Pick the strings in the order of which the numbers appear. For this song, it is strings 1 2 3 1 2 3.
Play this pattern 10-20 times until you can do it smoothly.

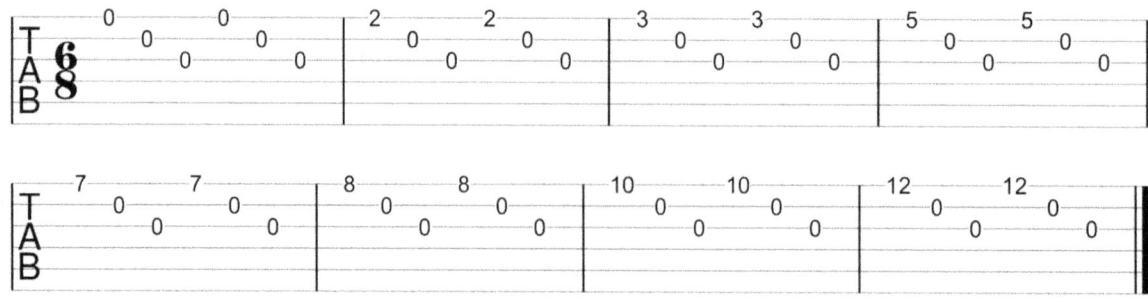

In the example above we are applying a *6-note picking pattern* to the E Natural Minor Scale. Here's how we recommend you learn this piece:

- Play the pattern twice on the open strings
- Move your first finger to the 2nd fret on string one and play the same picking pattern.
- Keep moving along each note of the scale until you get to fret 12.
- Repeat this three times.

Congratulations! You have now learned all of your fundamental skills!

Picking Study

Here is a short study piece that uses the picking skill along the first string. This piece will reinforce your picking skill and fretting technique while introducing you to learning longer pieces of music.

How to learn this piece.

- Say the first line three times, then play it three times.
- Say the second line three times, then play it three times.
- Say the third line three times, then play it three times.
- Say the fourth line three times, then play it three times.
- Now play from the start of the piece to the end of the piece three times.

When you practice this way you are training your brain to remember the numbers and not be reliant on reading every single note. This will result in more of your attention going towards your fingers and making sure they are performing the correct motions which will result in fewer mistakes and cleaner playing.

Of course, you can look up at the music for guidance whenever you need to.

Strumming Study

Here is a short study piece that uses our strumming skill combined with notes along the first string.

```
Line 1 (4/4):
  12        10         8          7
   0         0         0          0
   0         0         0          0

Line 2:
   8         7          5         3
   0         0          0         0
   0         0          0         0

Line 3:
  12        10          8         7
   0         0          0         0
   0         0          0         0

Line 4:
   5         3          2         0
   0         0          0         0
   0         0          0         0
```

How to Learn this Piece.

- Say the first line three times, then play it three times.
- Say the second line three times, then play it three times.
- Say the third line three times, then play it three times.
- Say the fourth line three times, then play it three times.
- Now play from the start of the piece to the end of the piece three times

Other Tips

Remember to let the notes ring out for four counts from the moment you strum before you release your finger and move to the next note.

Be mindful that your pick doesn't come to rest on the third string in anticipation of your strum, this will mute the string.

Picking Pattern Study

Here is a short study piece that uses a picking pattern along with notes on the first string.

Often the biggest challenge people have with picking pattern pieces is remembering the patterns and having to look between their hands each time they change string.

A great exercise to help overcome this is to focus on playing the pattern with your eyes shut. Play the pattern 3 times with your eyes open, then 3 times with your eyes shut. Open your eyes and play it another three times and then shut your eyes and try to get 5 times with your eyes shut. Open your eyes for 3 more times before trying to go 10 times in a row with your eyes shut. if you can do this, you won't need to look at your picking hand anymore.

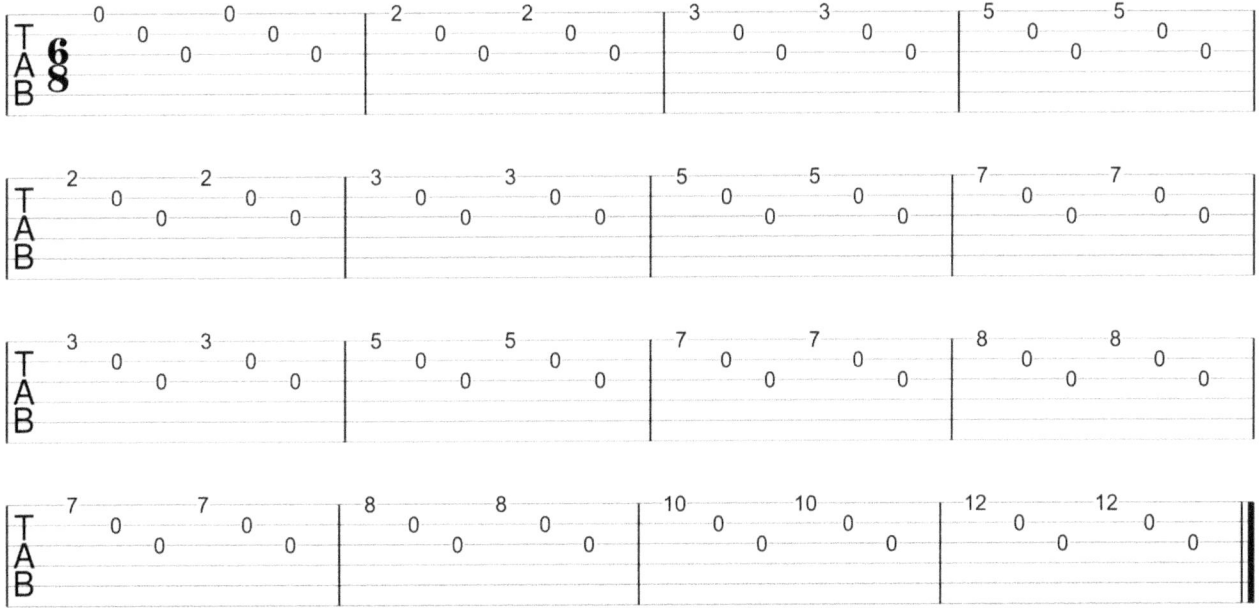

How to learn this piece.

- Say the first line three times, then play it three times (ignore the zeros).
- Say the second line three times, then play it three times.
- Say the third line three times, then play it three times.
- Say the fourth line three times, then play it three times.
- Now play from the start of the piece to the end of the piece three times.

Using Multiple Fingers

There are three patterns to help us decide which fingers to use.

Green | Blue | Red

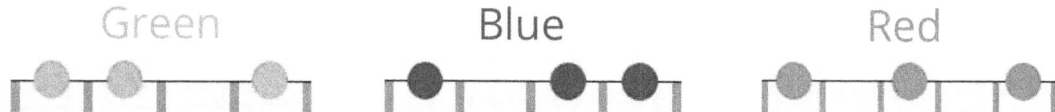

- The Green Pattern is a 4-fret stretch that we play with fingers 1 - 2 - 4
- The Blue Pattern is a 4-fret stretch that we play with fingers 1 - 3 - 4
- The Red Pattern is a 5-fret stretch that we play with fingers 1- 2 - 4

Use these three rules to help you decide which fingers to use within each pattern:

- Put your first finger on the lowest note,
- Put your pinkie finger on the highest note,
- Put either your second or third finger on the middle note as per the pattern you are playing.

1. **Frets 2 3 5** ________ Pattern ☐1 ☐2 ☐3 ☐4 ☐5
2. **Frets 3 5 7** ________ Pattern ☐1 ☐2 ☐3 ☐4 ☐5
3. **Frets 5 7 8** ________ Pattern ☐1 ☐2 ☐3 ☐4 ☐5
4. **Frets 7 8 10** ________ Pattern ☐1 ☐2 ☐3 ☐4 ☐5
5. **Frets 8 10 12** ________ Pattern ☐1 ☐2 ☐3 ☐4 ☐5

First Playthrough Any Fingers | **Three In A Row Correct Fingers** | **Ten In A Row Correct Fingers** | **Eyes Shut Three In A Row** | **All 6 String Correct Fingers**

5 complete | 10 complete | 15 complete | 20 complete | 25 Complete Level Up!

Red - Green - Blue Fragment Exercises

These simple exercises are great for developing the co-ordination of your fretting hand so that you can play using multiple fingers with ease.

Assign 1 finger per fret as per the *Red, Green & Blue Patterns* and focus on smoothly transitioning from note to note.

1 = First Playthrough.   2 = 3x   3 = 10x   4 = All 6 Strings 3x   5 = Connect All Three 10x

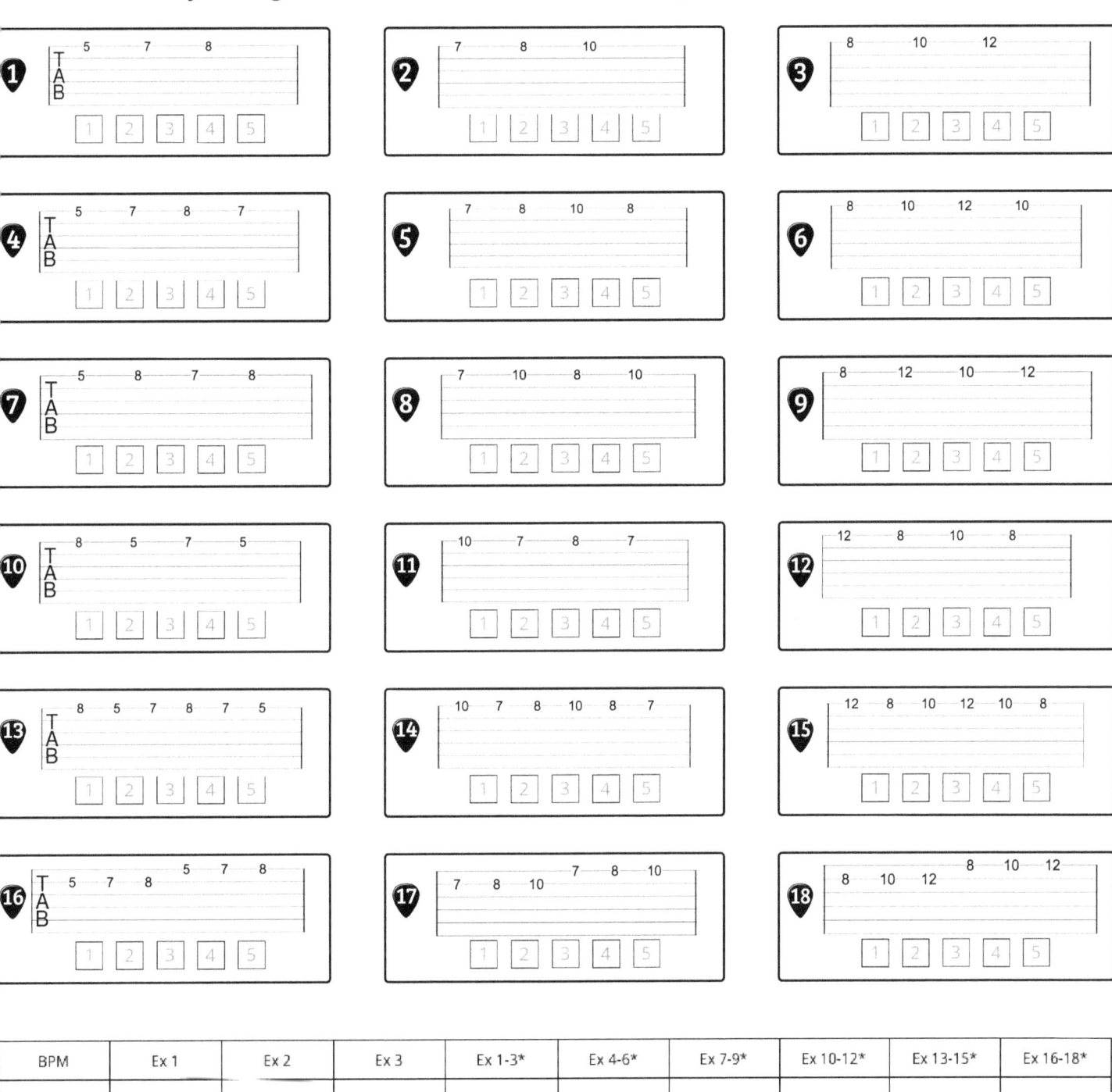

*Combine 3 Fragments into a longer exercise

What Next?

Congratulations! You've completed the **Getting Into Guitar** section and should now have a solid understanding of all your basic skills!

In the next chapter, you'll find 15 study pieces that will further develop your Picking, Strumming, and Picking Pattern skills.

You can also start looking at the **Riffs Section** which will introduce you to some basic rhythm guitar playing and real songs to add to your repertoire.

Following that, there's a section dedicated to **Memorizing The Fretboard**. Here you'll delve into notes and scales, deepening your understanding of the guitar's fretboard and how it works.

Lastly, we introduce the **Level-Up System**, which teaches you how to play along with any song. You'll learn how to navigate songs and chord progressions and start building up your repertoire of pieces to play.

While you can work through this book in a linear way, we typically recommend dividing your time like this: Spend 30% of your practice time on study pieces, another 30% on improving your fretboard knowledge and technical skills, and the remaining 30% on songs and repertoire in the level-up section.

Use the remaining 10% of your practice time however you like. Have fun exploring YouTube lessons, watching videos on our Guitar Dojo Online platform, creating your own music, or revisiting something you've previously learned.

If you haven't already, I highly recommend logging into the online course that accompanies this method book. There, you'll find video lessons, demonstrations, recommended learning pathways, and practice routines that will help you follow this method in a more structured way.

Enjoy your guitar journey!

Section 2

Study Pieces

In this section, you'll discover 15 study pieces to enhance your skills. These pieces are divided into five single-note exercises, five strumming exercises, and five picking pattern exercises. They're designed to help you build upon your fundamental skills.

While you can progress through these pieces in a step-by-step order, I recommend learning one piece from each category simultaneously. This balanced approach helps you develop a well-rounded skill set.

You'll find clear, step-by-step instructions for learning and practising each piece. Additionally, there are additional levels to explore once you've mastered the basics.

For extra guidance, you can watch video demonstrations of each piece in the accompanying online course to this book.

Picking Study 1: The Major Scale

Earlier in this book you learned 8 notes along string number 1.

While you didn't know it at the time, you learned your very first scale - The Natural Minor Scale!

In this lesson, you will learn the Major Scale which is the foundation of all Western Music.

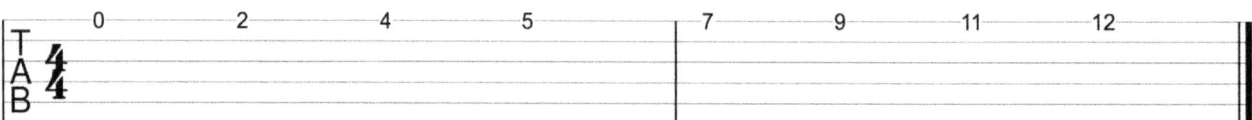

Use the **Say It Three Times, Play It Three Times** method to learn and practice the Major Scale along on string 1. Notice how it sounds and feels different to the minor scale you learned previously.

Major Scale Study Piece

Once you have learned the major scale above you can put it into practice with a brand-new study piece composed in the Key of E Major on string 1. Note that this piece uses several different rhythms so pay attention to which notes ring out for longer.

Tip: From here on the study pieces will get longer and more challenging. To make learning easier break each line into individual bars, learn each bar separately and then put them together before moving on to the next line. This is called the **Chain Method**.

Picking Study 2: Skipping Notes

Our next study piece will continue to use the E Major Scale on String 1.

This time we will be skipping notes in order to challenge your ability to change between notes smoothly.

You may wish to work on switching between two individual notes in isolation several times until it becomes smooth before you move on to the next notes.

This means that the 8 notes in the first line could be divided up into 4 chunks of two notes each, then two chunks of four notes, before putting the entire line together.

How to learn this piece.

- Say and play the first two notes three times each.
- Say and play the next two notes three times each.
- Say and play all four notes in the first bar three times each.
- Repeat steps 1-3 for the second bar on the first line.
- Put the entire first line together and play it three times.
- Repeat this process for all four lines before putting the entire piece together

Picking Study 3: Changing Direction

For this piece, we are returning to the E Natural Minor Scale on String 1 which uses the frets 0 2 3 5 7 8 10 12.

We will be using a combination of rhythms while playing a melody that ascends (goes from low notes to high notes) and descends (high to low) in different directions.

Once again, learn the piece bar-by-bar before putting it all together.

Additional Levels

Try some of these additional levels to make the piece more challenging.

- Play the song as written on a single string.
- Try playing the same notes but on a different string.
- Try strumming the longer notes (include strings 2 & 3).
- Try strumming every note.
- Make up your own picking pattern for the piece.
- Convert the piece from E Minor to E Major by changing the 3's to 4's and the 8's to 9's.

Picking Study 4: A Day In The Sun

The melody for this piece is played on the third string and has been composed using the Major Scale.

You should identify which of the three RGB Patterns should be used for each bar and practice each phrase in isolation.

You should also start learning the piece two bars at a time as the phrases are longer and contain more notes. Note that while guitar tabs don't offer us the rhythm, each bar must add up to 4 counts and the number of notes in each bar along with the spaces give us an indication of which notes need to ring out for longer.

```
|-4/4--0---4---2---4---|--0-------0-------|--2---5---4---5---|--2-------2-------|
|----------------------|------------------|------------------|------------------|
|----------------------|------------------|------------------|------------------|

|------7---5---4-------|--7---5---4-------|--2---2---4---4---|--0---------------|
|----------------------|------------------|------------------|------------------|
|----------------------|------------------|------------------|------------------|

|------0---4---2---4---|--0-------4-------|--2---5---4---5---|--2-------5-------|
|----------------------|------------------|------------------|------------------|
|----------------------|------------------|------------------|------------------|

|------7---5---4---5---|--7---5---4---5---|--4---4---2---2---|--0---------------||
|----------------------|------------------|------------------|------------------||
|----------------------|------------------|------------------|------------------||
```

Additional Levels

Try some of these additional levels to make the piece more challenging.

- Play the song as written on a single string.
- Try playing the same notes but on a different string.
- Try strumming the longer notes (include strings 1 & 2).
- Try strumming every note (include strings 1 & 2).
- Try adding your own picking pattern to the piece.
- Convert the piece from G Major to G Minor by changing the 4's to 3's.

Picking Study 5: Building Blocks

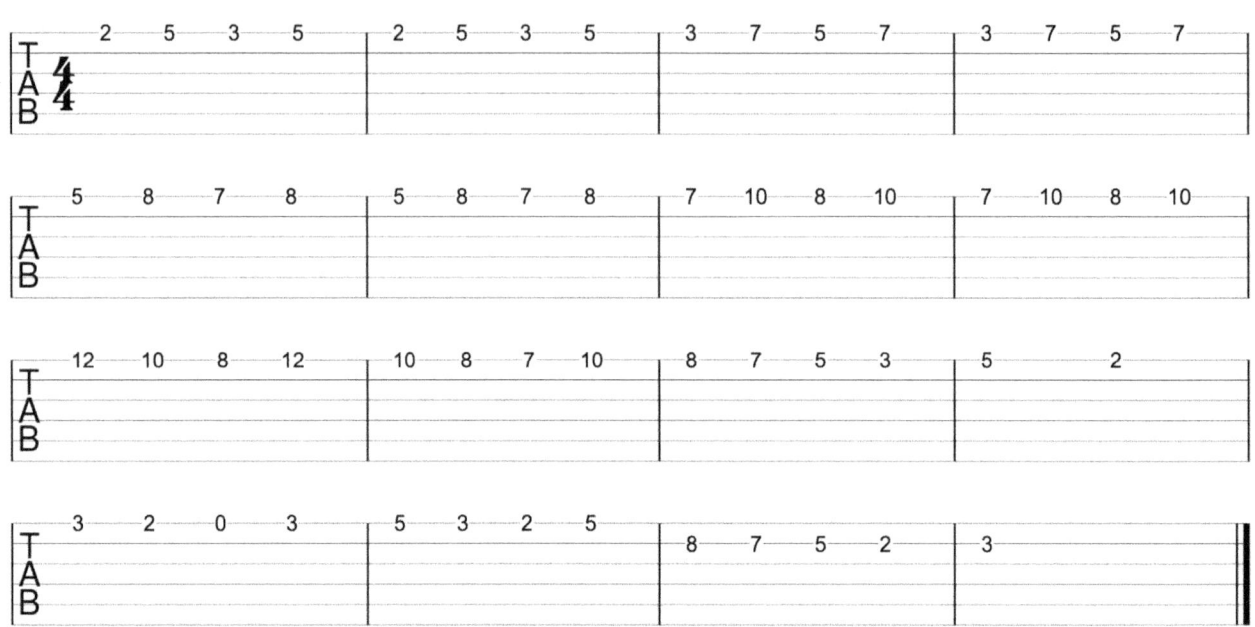

Practice Tips

Before you start playing this piece, identify which of the three RGB Patterns (Red, Green, or Blue shapes) are being used for each bar of music.

Once you have identified the best finger pattern to use, practice each bar in isolation before piecing them together. Whenever there is an open string do not include the '0' as the lowest note.

For example, in bar 13 you will use your first finger on fret 2 and your second finger on fret 3. No finger is needed to play the 0.

Additional Levels

Try some of these additional levels to make the piece more challenging.

- Play with all downstrokes.
- Play with all upstrokes.
- Play with alternate picking.
- Try 'Double Picking' every note for extra synchronization practice.
- Apply a different sequence to the melody (but use the same RGB patterns).

Strumming Study 1: One Finger Minor Blues

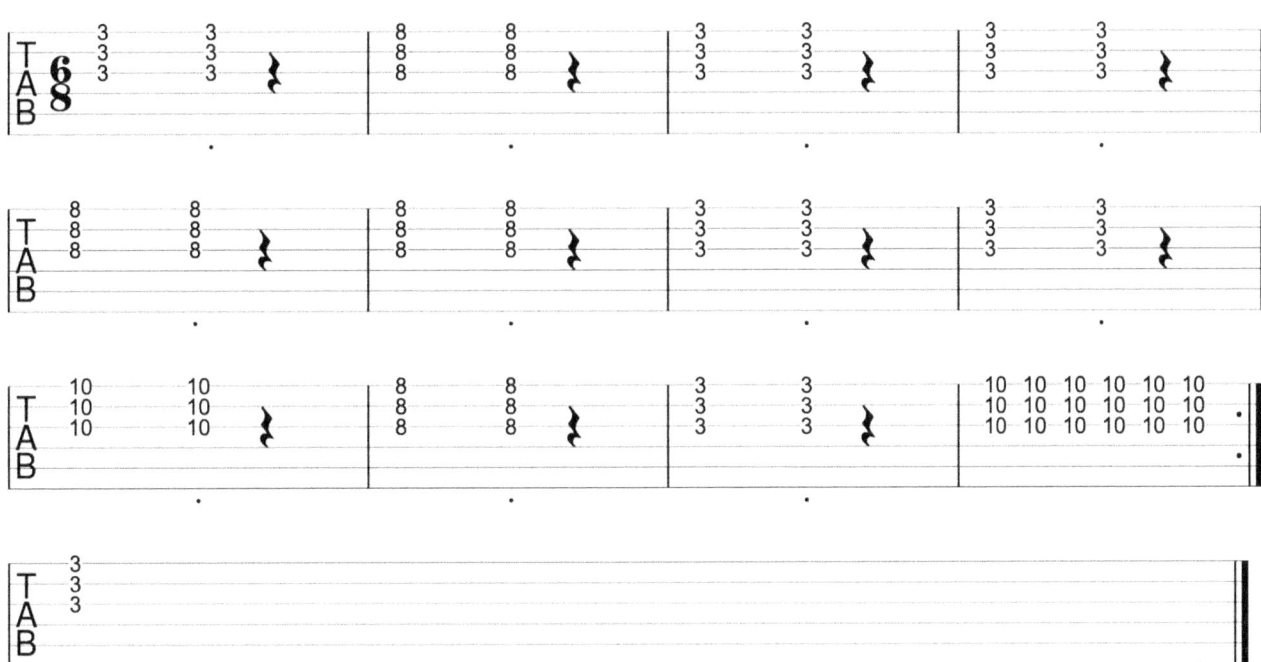

Practice Tips
Place your first finger across the first three strings at fret 3 and squeeze hard enough for all three strings to ring out when strummed together. If you are struggling to make the notes work you can put your second finger on top of your first finger for extra leverage. You could also use three different fingers if need be. When it comes time to play fret number 8 or fret number 10 hold the same shape and move your finger shape to the new position. You may wish to practice clapping the rhythm to get the timing right.

Notes
- You can repeat the piece (bars 1-12) as many times as you like before finishing at fret 3 with a final strum.
- The piece is in 6/8 timing, this means you count to 6 and strum on beats 1 & 4.

Additional Levels
- Try different strumming patterns within the 6/8 time signature
- Turn the piece into a major blues by playing the same shapes one string lower.
- Use a different inversion of your minor chord for a different-sounding minor blues.
- Transpose the piece to a new key

Strumming Study 2: Busking At The Market

Practice Tips

There is a lot of information here so you will benefit from learning each bar in isolation and putting them all together three times before moving onto the next line. It will take more work upfront but will save you time spent relearning the piece in future practice sessions.

Additional Levels

- Learn the piece as a single string melody
- Pluck with your thumb and first two fingers instead of strumming with a pick.
- Try strumming with your thumb only
- Try creating your own piece by combining the notes 0 2 3 5 7 8 10 12 on string 1 with the open 2nd & 3rd string.

Strumming Study 3: One Finger Major Blues

```
T |-2-------------| |-7-------------| |-2-------------| |-2-------------|
A |4/4 -2---------| |-7-------------| |-2-------------| |-2-------------|
B |-2-------------| |-7-------------| |-2-------------| |-2-------------|

T |-7-------------| |-7-------------| |-2-------------| |-2-------------|
A |-7-------------| |-7-------------| |-2-------------| |-2-------------|
B |-7-------------| |-7-------------| |-2-------------| |-2-------------|

T |-9-------------| |-7-------------| |-2-------------| |-9--9--9--9---:||
A |-9-------------| |-7-------------| |-2-------------| |-9--9--9--9---:||
B |-9-------------| |-7-------------| |-2-------------| |-9--9--9--9----||

T |-2-------------||
A |-2-------------||
B |-2-------------||
```

Practice Tips

Place your first finger across Strings 2, 3 & 4 at fret 2 and squeeze hard enough for all three strings to ring out when strummed together. If you are struggling to make the notes work you can put your second finger on top of your first finger for extra leverage or use three different fingers. When it comes time to play fret 7 or 9 simply move the same shape to the new position.

Notes

- You can repeat the piece (bars 1-12) as many times as you like before finishing at fret 2 with a final strum.
- The piece is in 4/4 time, strum accordingly.

Additional Levels

- Try different strumming patterns within the 4/4 time signature
- Turn the piece into a minor blues by playing the same shapes one string higher.
- Use a different inversion of your minor chord for a different-sounding minor blues.
- Transpose the piece to a new key

Strumming Study 4: Medieval Fair

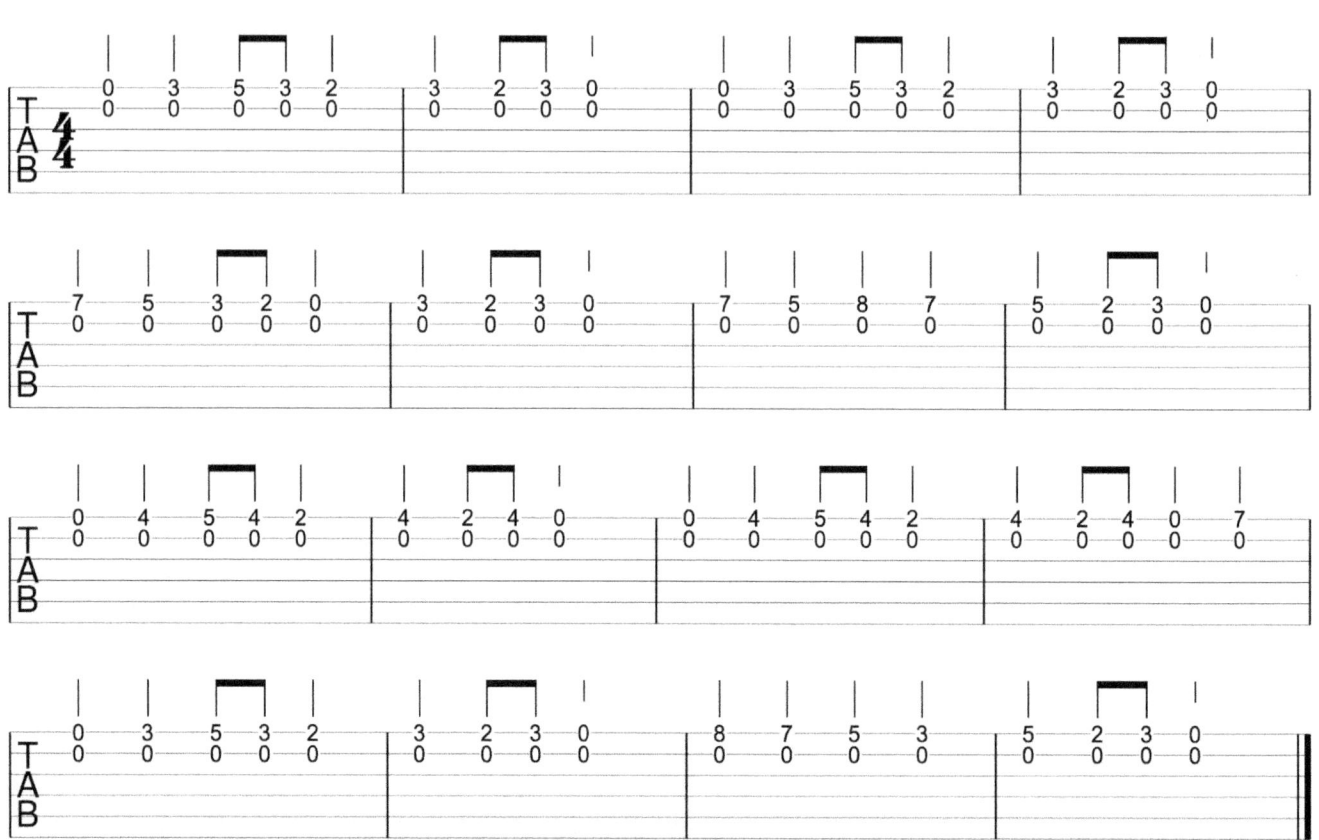

Practice Tips

Use the rhythmic notation to get the timing right and practice clapping the rhythms before you add the melody on the guitar. While the fret numbers might change, the rhythm patterns repeat fairly consistently throughout the piece. The Red/Green/Blue patterns will work for the majority of bars.

Additional Levels
- Play the piece on string 1 using picking only instead of strumming
- Use multiple fingers

Strumming Study 5: One Finger Shuffle Blues

```
T |---------------------------|---------------------------|---------------------------|---------------------------|
A |  2 2 4 4 2 2 4 4          |  2 2 4 4 2 2 4 4          |  2 2 4 4 2 2 4 4          |  2 2 4 4 2 2 4 4          |
B |  0 0 0 0 0 0 0 0          |  0 0 0 0 0 0 0 0          |  0 0 0 0 0 0 0 0          |  0 0 0 0 0 0 0 0          |

T |---------------------------|---------------------------|---------------------------|---------------------------|
A |  2 2 4 4 2 2 4 4          |  2 2 4 4 2 2 4 4          |  2 2 4 4 2 2 4 4          |  2 2 4 4 2 2 4 4          |
B |  0 0 0 0 0 0 0 0          |  0 0 0 0 0 0 0 0          |  0 0 0 0 0 0 0 0          |  0 0 0 0 0 0 0 0          |

T |---------------------------|---------------------------|---------------------------|---------------------------|
A |                           |  2 2 4 4 2 2 4 4          |  2 2 4 4 2 2 4 4          |                           |
B |  2 2 4 4 2 2 4 4          |  0 0 0 0 0 0 0 0          |  0 0 0 0 0 0 0 0          |  2 2 4 4 2 2 4 4          |
  |  0 0 0 0 0 0 0 0          |                           |                           |  0 0 0 0 0 0 0 0          |

T |---------------------------|
A |  2                        |
B |  0                        |
```

Practice Tips

This song is based on a two-fret repeating riff which is moved to three different strings following the **12 Bar Blues** chord progression.

To play the riff, place your first finger on string four, fret 2, and strum twice. Then move your finger up to fret 4 and strum two more times. Practice getting used to moving between these two frets until you can do it smoothly and consistently. Then repeat the same movements on the third and fifth strings.

Memorizing the progression, and knowing when to change the riff to a new string will make the transitions easier.

Notes

- You can repeat the piece (bars 1-12) as many times as you like and when you're ready to finish just strum the final A5 chord with a final strum to end the piece.

Additional Levels

- Use your third finger to play fret 4, so you don't have to move your entire hand.
- Try using both a straight rhythm, and a shuffle rhythm. Which do you like more?
- Ask your teacher about playing this piece using blues shuffle chords on strings 5 & 6.
- You can add a blues lick to the last bar of each line for more impressive playing.

Pattern Study 1: Memories

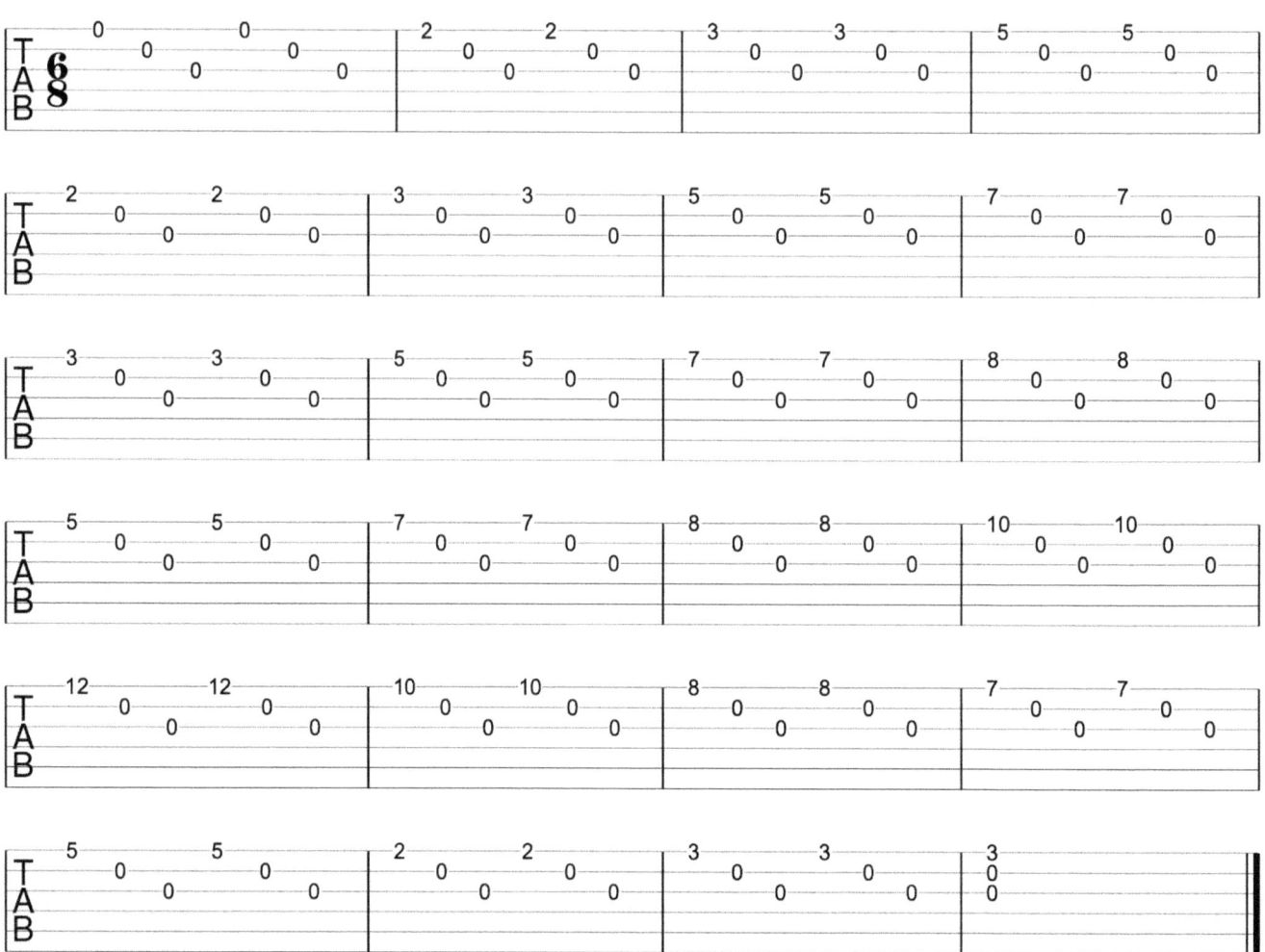

Practice Tips

While it looks like there's lots of information on this page, it can easily be reduced to a group of 4 numbers per line with a 6-note picking pattern.

Practice the picking pattern in isolation until it becomes comfortable, then add in the fretted notes. Remember to say the fretted note numbers three times before you play them three times each so that you more easily commit them to memory.

Additional Levels

- Try playing the piece with your fingers instead of using a guitar pick
- Reverse the picking pattern to go 3 2 1 3 2 1.
- You can try strumming instead of picking.
- Compose your own piece of music by rearranging the order of the notes, or trying a different strumming pattern.

Pattern Study 2: The Garden

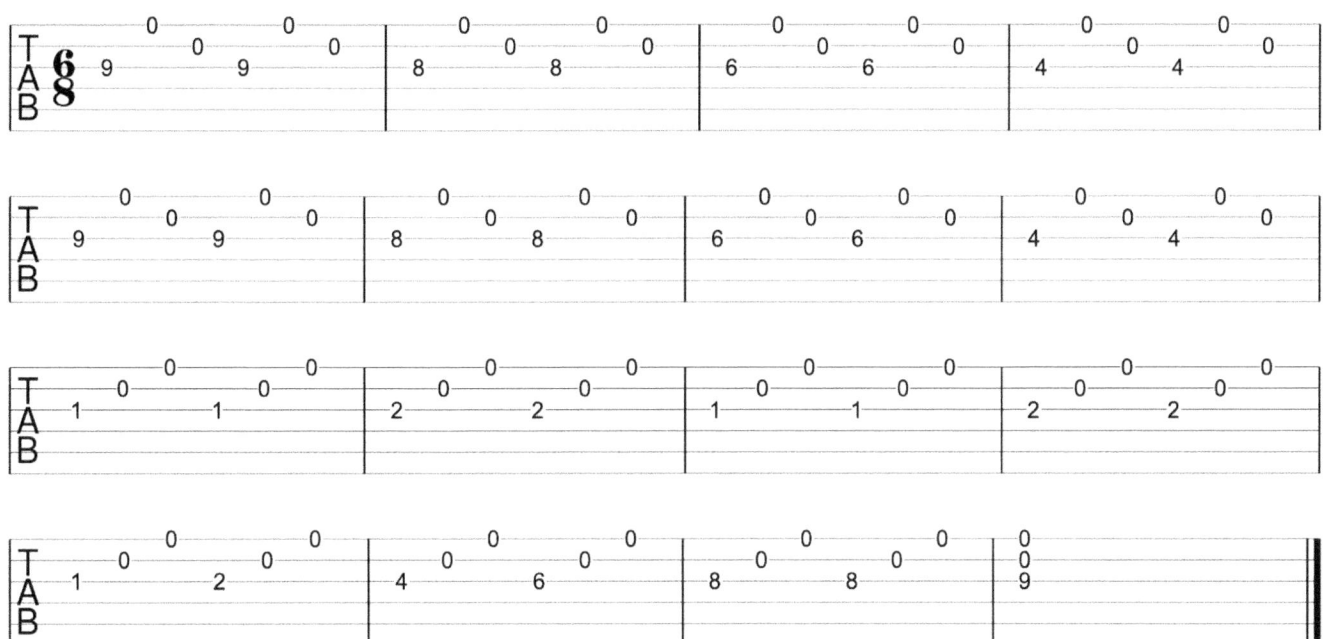

Practice Tips

Start by learning the song as a melody along string 3.

When you get the hang of it you can add in the picking pattern.

Commit the picking patterns to memory and practice them until they become comfortable. For the melody use your first and second fingers exclusively, change fingers whenever the notes are a semitone apart.

Additional Levels

- Play the piece as a single-string melody.
- Use the first picking pattern for the entire song.
- Use the second picking pattern for the entire song.
- Try strumming instead of picking.
- Try transposing the melody to a minor key by changing the 6's to 5's and the 8's to 7's.

Pattern Study 3: Teeter Totter

This picking study ascends and descends using a simple, sequential linear melody. While our fretting hand will have an easy job, our picking hand is going to have its work cut out for it.

The piece incorporates string skipping and will have your picking hand bouncing from string 1 to 3 with the intention of not hitting string two as it 'skips' over. Depending on whether you start with a down or an upstroke, you'll be training an *outside picking* motion, or an *inside picking* motion.

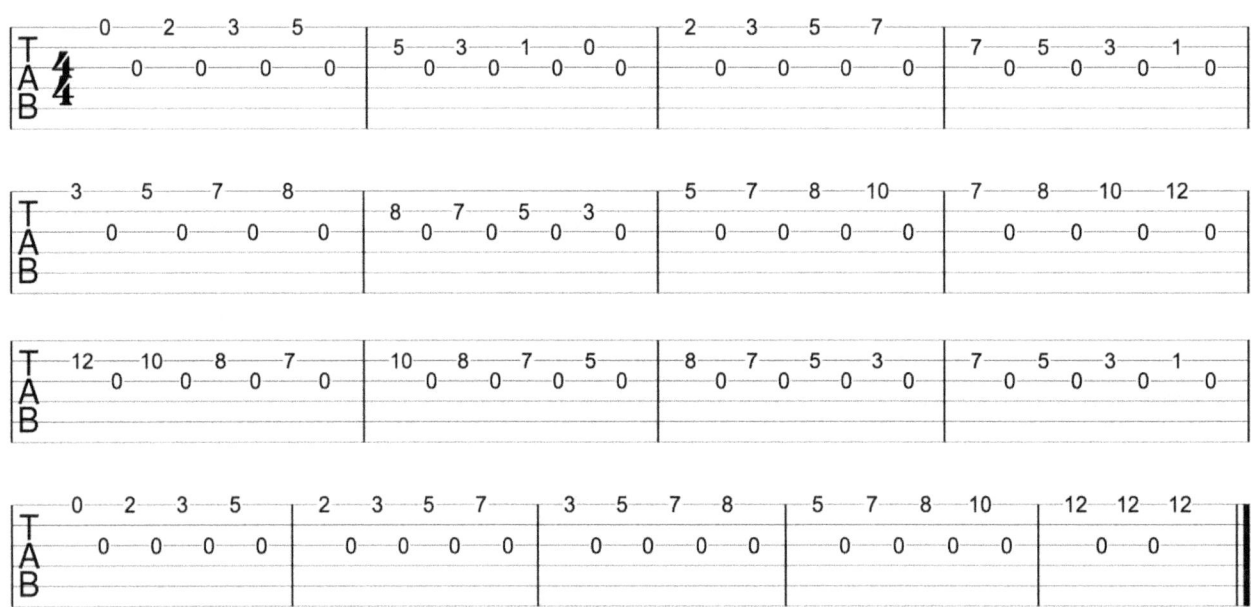

Practice Tips
Start by learning the song as a melody along strings 1 & 2 When you get the hang of it you can add in the picking pattern.

You want to use a small '*figure 8*' motion (∞) to pick inside of the strings. When playing a bar that involves skipping over string 2 you will need to dip the pick in and out to avoid hitting string two. The motion is the same when you're playing two adjacent strings, just smaller as you don't need to skip over any strings.

Additional Levels
- Play the piece as a single-string melody without any open strings.
- Start with an upstroke and play the piece using '*outside picking*'.
- Start with a downstroke and play the piece using '*inside picking*'.

Pattern Study 4: Tirisfal Glades

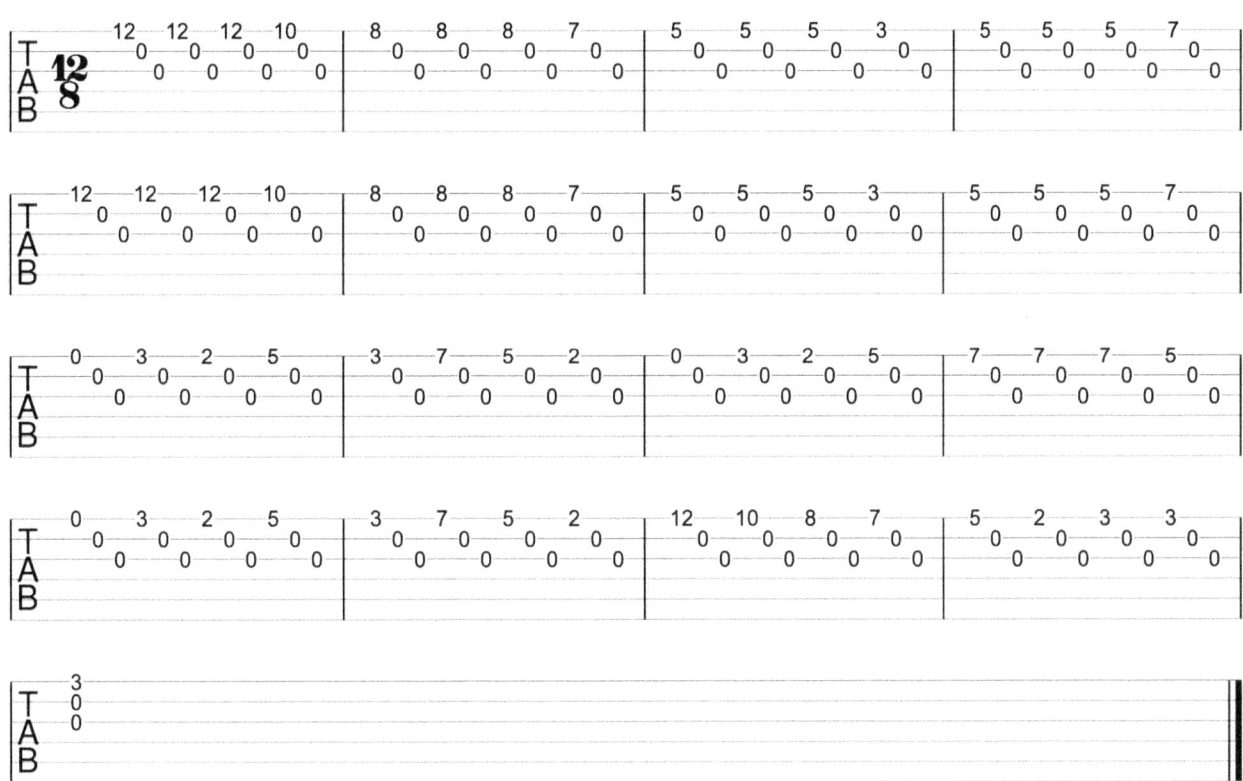

Practice Tips

This piece is going to challenge your memory by adding lots of additional notes and odd groupings within each bar. Look for patterns where you can to reduce the amount of information you're dealing with.

Learn the melody first then come back in and add the picking pattern.

Additional Levels

- Play the piece as a single-string melody without any picking pattern.
- Use an *'up-up-down'* picking pattern.
- Use a *'down-up-up'* picking pattern.
- Try strumming instead of picking.

Pattern Study 5: Six Strings

Our final study piece sounds very full as it includes the 6th string in the picking pattern allowing for all the notes to resonate with each other.

It's important to practice the picking pattern in isolation before attempting to apply it to the rest of the piece.

Remember, just say the number that changes in each bar (0 2 3 5, 7 5 8 7 etc) and apply the picking pattern.

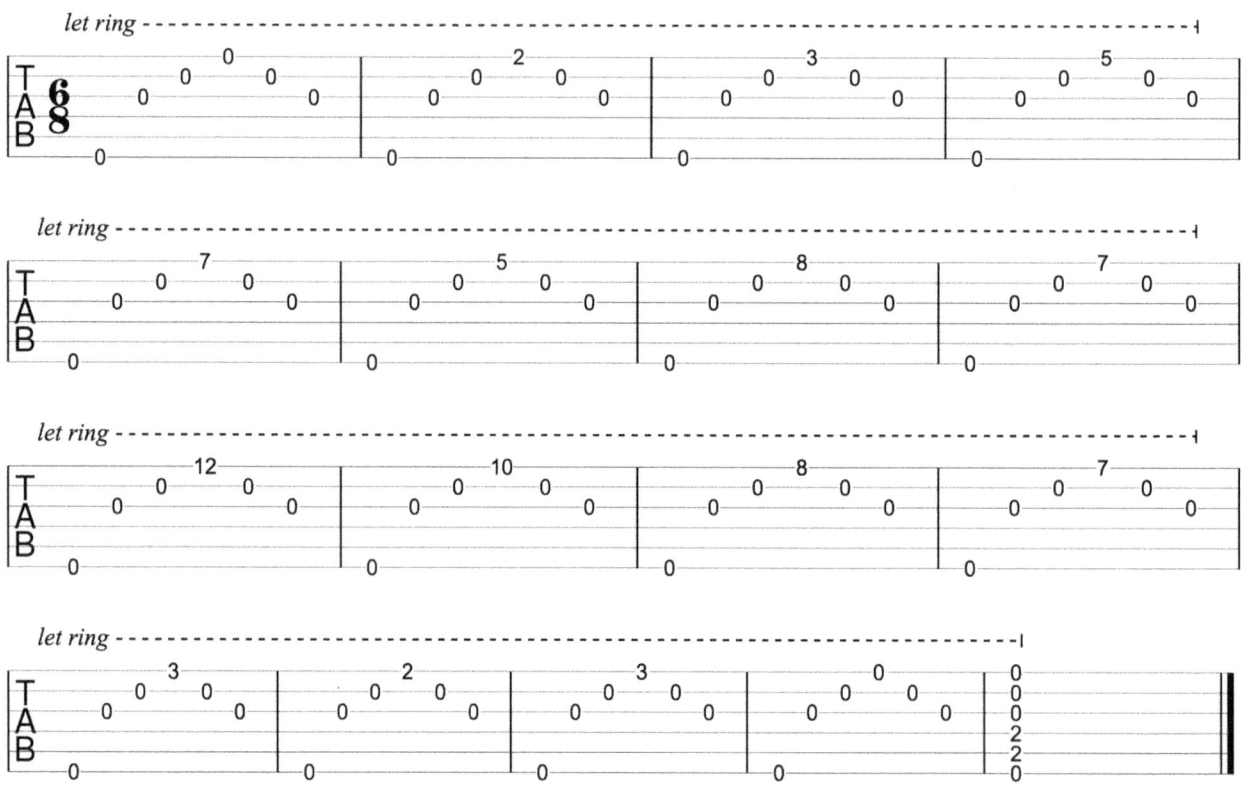

How To Learn This Piece

- Practice the picking pattern (6 3 2 1 2 3) in isolation until you can play it smoothly without mistakes
- Apply the picking pattern to the first four numbers (0 2 3 5) three times.
- Apply the picking pattern to the next four numbers (7 5 8 7) three times.
- Apply the picking pattern to the next four numbers (12 10 8 7) three times.
- Apply the picking pattern to the last four numbers (3 2 3 0) three times.
- Put it all together and finish with an Em chord strummed on all 6 strings.

Section 3

Riffs

Riffs are short, repeated patterns of music that are usually played on the thicker strings.

They're great to learn because they are easy, help improve our timing, and will be instantly recognizable by anyone listening to you play them!

By learning different riffs, you'll be able to play them confidently and impress your friends and family with your guitar skills!

So, let's start learning some cool riffs that you can show off to everyone!

Lesson 16 - An Introduction To Riffs

A **riff** is a short, repeated pattern of music usually played on the lower strings of the guitar. It is often associated with the most memorable part of the song. If I tell you to think of '*Smoke on the Water*' or "*Back In Black*' chances are you can already hear the riff in your head.

We like to teach our students riffs for 3 reasons:

- They are easy and lots of fun to play
- They help you develop your timing and rhythm skills
- You can show them off to people straight away.

To learn riffs, we apply the *say it three times, play it three times* process to saying the notes and clapping the rhythm to get the feel for the riff before playing it on the guitar.

Let's take a look at the riff to **Hit The Road Jack** below:

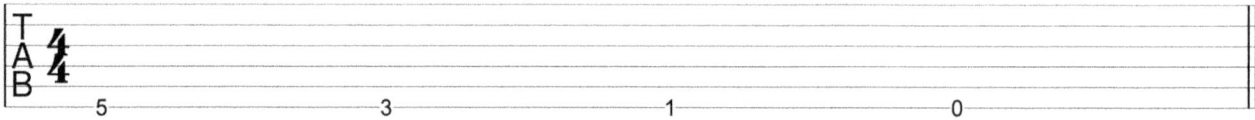

A quick look at the riff above tells us that we are playing on string 6 and that we are only playing four notes: fret 5, fret 3, fret 1 and the open string.

How You Should Learn This Riff

- Listen to the song so you know what the riff sounds like
- Clap along to the riff to internalise the rhythm.
- Clap along to the riff while saying the fret numbers aloud to memorise them.
- Play the riff on your guitar.

By definition, Riffs are repeating patterns of music so make sure you play the riff you are working on at least 10 times in a row before you move on to a new one.

Learning Tip: More complex riffs can be broken into chunks and pieced together like any other musical example

Lesson 17 - Classic Rock Riffs

Here are 5 easy riffs to get you started. Don't forget to use the process we outlined on the previous page to help you learn and master each riff.

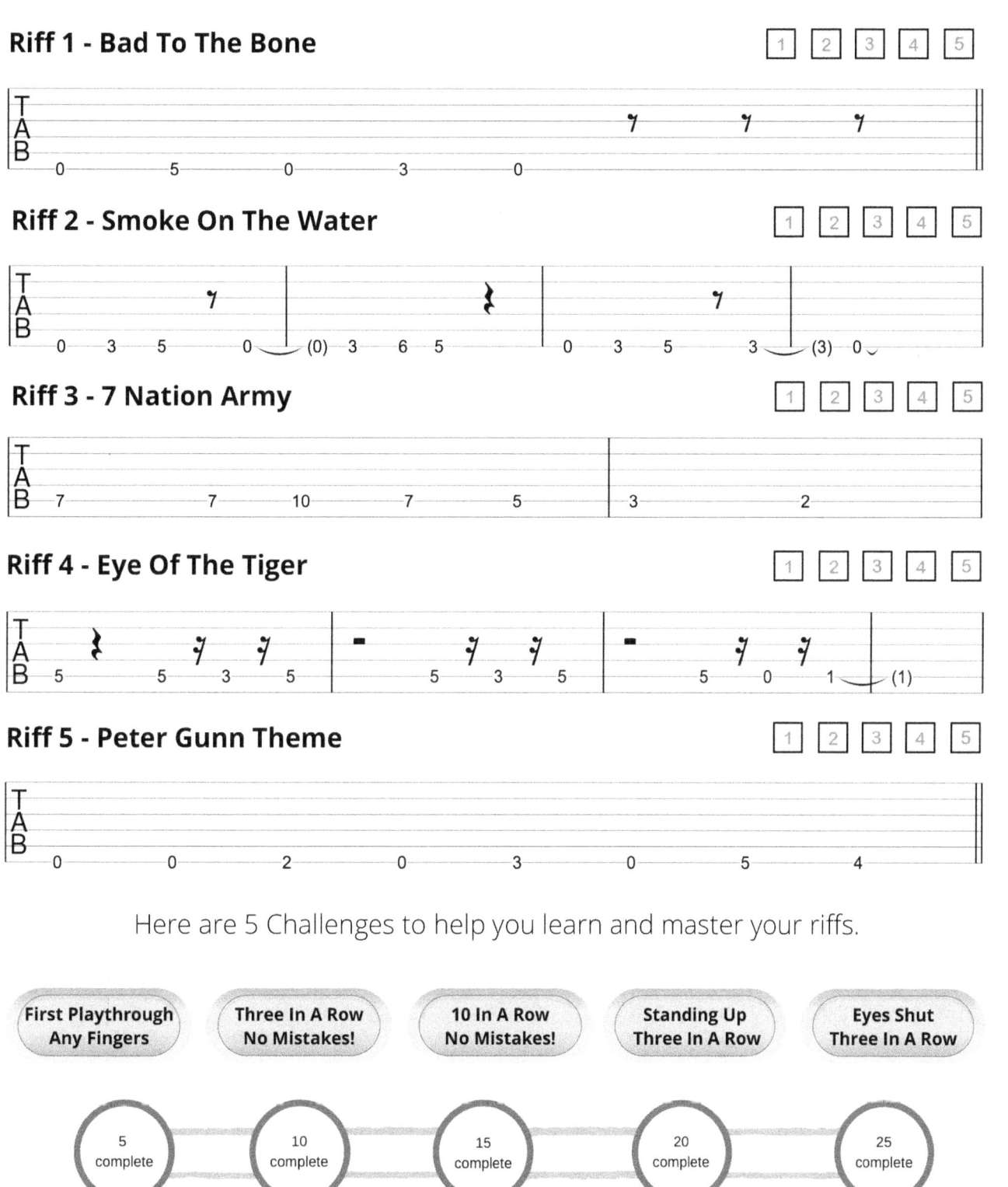

Here are 5 Challenges to help you learn and master your riffs.

Lesson 18 - Easy Modern Riffs

Here are 5 more contemporary riffs that you're bound to recognise.

Riff 1 - Believer 1 2 3 4 5

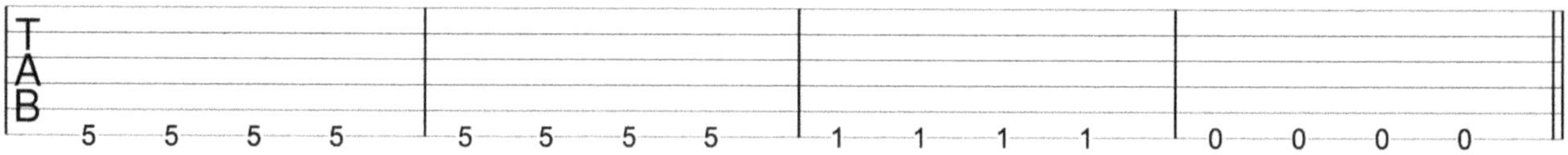

TAB
5 5 5 5
5 5 5 5
1 1 1 1
0 0 0 0

Riff 2 - Shake It Off 1 2 3 4 5

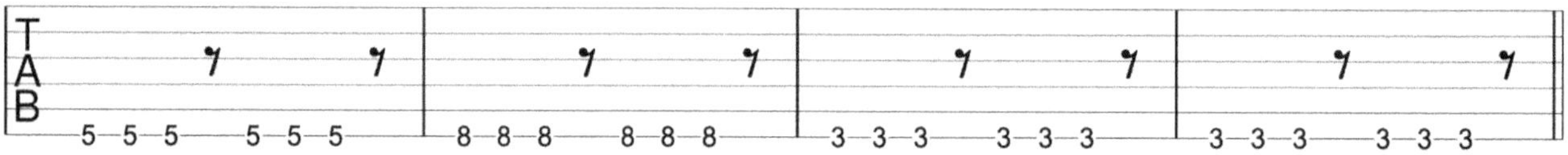

TAB
5-5-5 5-5-5
8-8-8 8-8-8
3-3-3 3-3-3
3-3-3 3-3-3

Riff 3 - Brutal 1 2 3 4 5

TAB
7 7 7 7 7 6 5

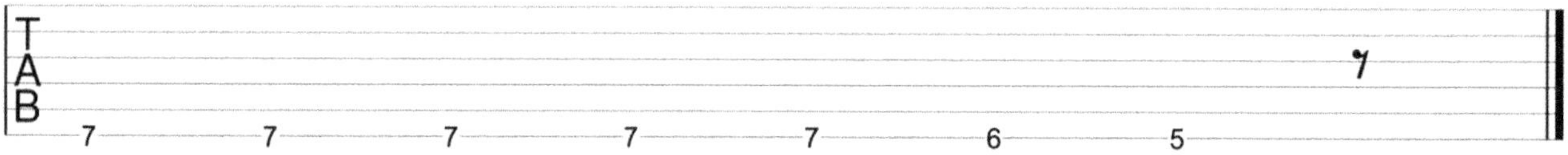

Riff 4 - Uptown Funk 1 2 3 4 5

TAB
5 5
10 8 5 10 8 4

Riff 5 - Castle On The Hill 1 2 3 4 5

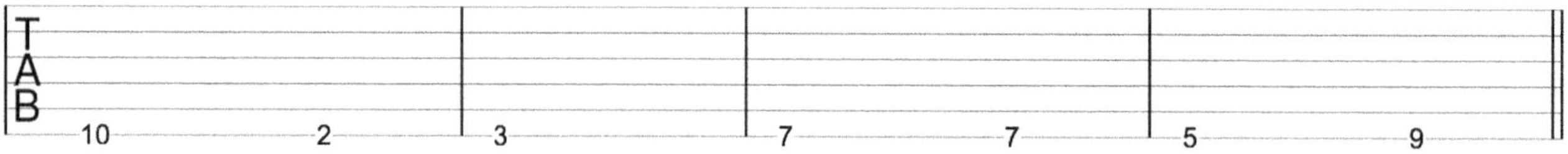

TAB
10 2
3
7 7
5 9

Tip: In addition to the regular riff challenges below, you can also try playing your riffs using Power Chords.

First Playthrough Any Fingers	Three In A Row No Mistakes!	10 In A Row No Mistakes!	Standing Up Three In A Row	Eyes Shut Three In A Row

5 complete — 10 complete — 15 complete — 20 complete — 25 complete

Level Up!

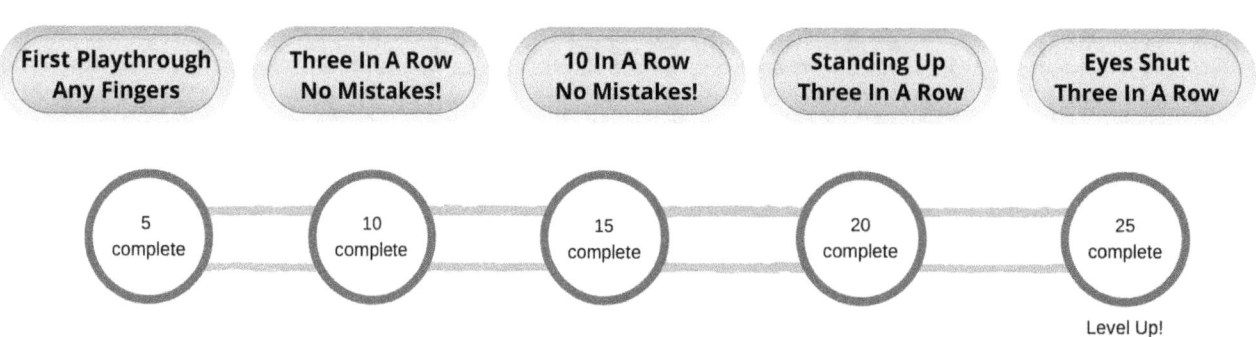

Section 5

Fretboard Memorisation

Learning the Fretboard is a very important yet often overlooked area of guitar playing.

Knowing where the notes are, and how they can be arranged into scales and chords will give you a comprehensive understanding of how the guitar works and will provide a solid foundation for you to draw from later when you start exploring music theory.

The better you know your fretboard, the better you know your guitar. It is after all, a pattern-based instrument and a little bit of knowledge as to how this works goes a long way towards your understanding of the instrument.

Plus, with the right tools it's really easy to memorise the fretboard!

Fretboard Memorisation

It is essential that you know where all the notes are located across the fretboard. You can use 3 rules to help you learn the notes along any string:

Rule 1 - The Musical Alphabet is made up of the notes 'A B C D E F & G'. After G it starts again at A
Rule 2 - The notes 'B & C' and 'E & F' are 'buddy notes'. Every other note has a 1 fret gap
Rule 3 - The same note repeats every 12 frets

Use the challenges to help you learn the notes along each of the 6 strings:

1 = Say It - 2 = Play It Forward 3x - 3 = Backwards 3x - 4 = Draw It From Memory - 5 = Say It From Memory

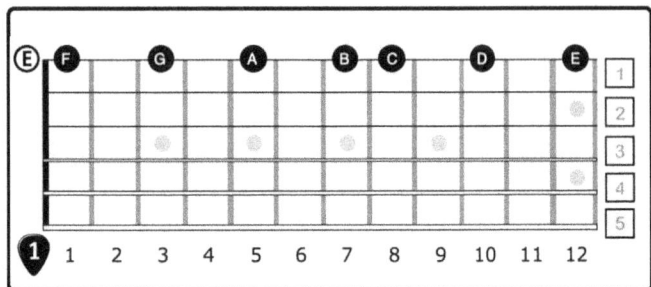
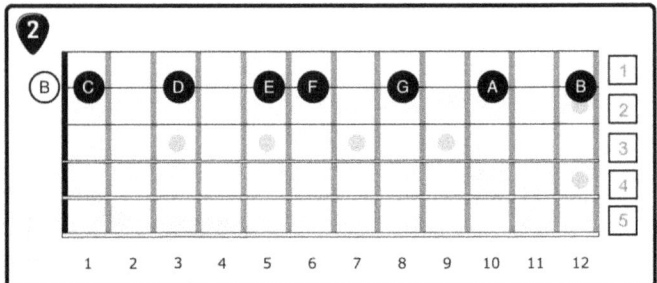
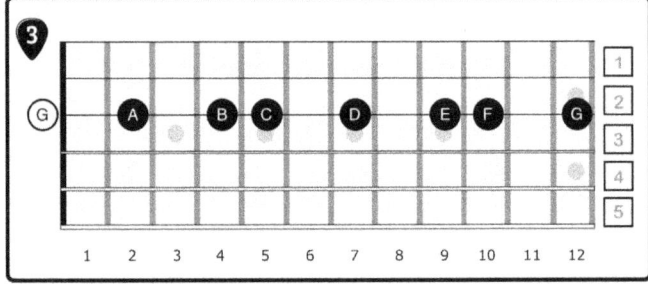
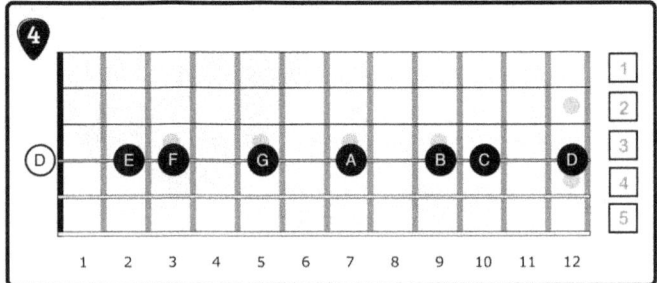
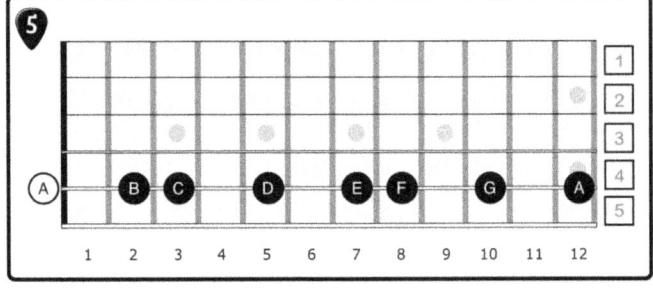
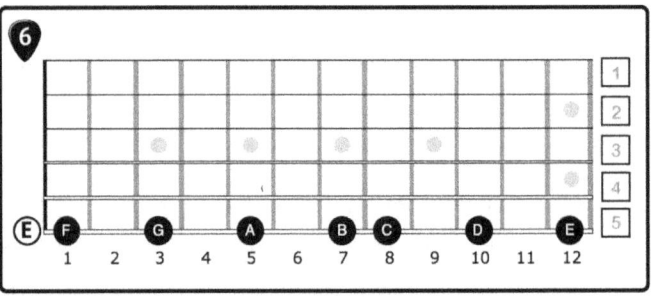

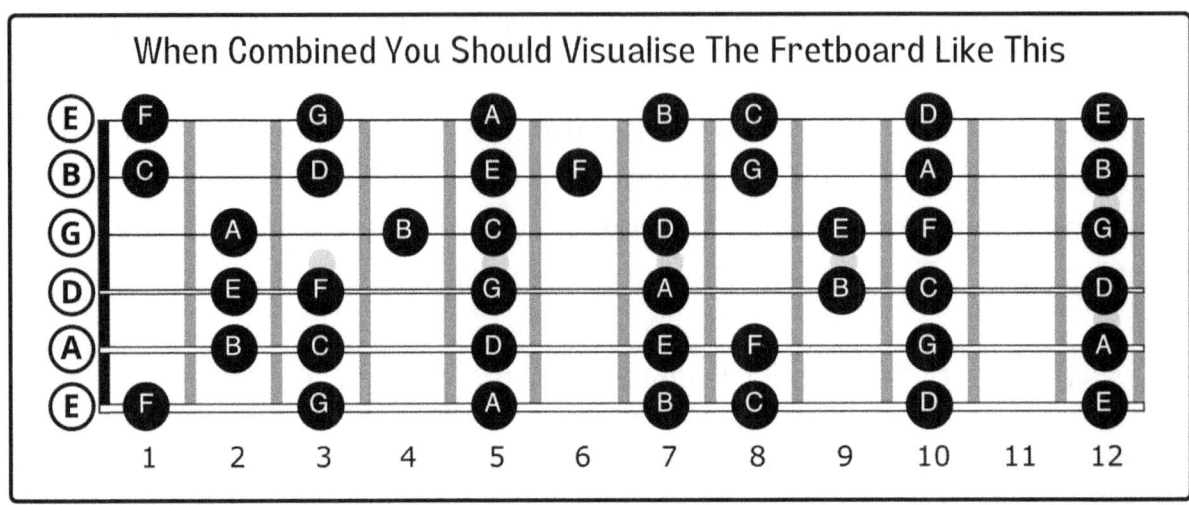

When Combined You Should Visualise The Fretboard Like This

© Melbourne Guitar Academy
www.MelbourneGuitarAcademy.com

Creating Bass Lines

When you look up songs on the internet you will likely be given song charts that are made up of lyrics and accompanying chords.

When you know how the fretboard is laid out, you can take any chord progression and turn it into a baseline. This is the foundation of the entire **Level-Up System**, upon which all your other chords can be built.

To complete each exercise, find where the notes are located on string six and write down the fret where they are found. You can do the same on string five before coming up with the most efficient combination of both strings.

1 = String 6   2 = String 5   3 = Most Efficient String Combo

1. C - G - Am - F
2. D - A - Bm - G
3. G - D - Em - C
4. A - E - F#m - D
5. E - B - C#m - A
6. F - C - Dm - Bb
7. Bb - F - Gm - Eb
8. Eb - Bb - cm - Ab
9. Ab - Eb - Fm - Db
10. F# - C# - D#m - B

Tips: Remember that # = +1 and ♭ = -1. You can also use the letters A & E to indicate which string frets are on when combining both strings.

HORIZONTAL SCALES

A Scale is a collection of notes arranged in a particular pattern. This pattern is known as the *Scale Formula* and is responsible for a scale sounding a particular way. Think of the scale formula as a recipe that you follow to create a specific sound.

Traditionally, scales are played vertically across all 6 strings. We will start by learning how to play them horizontally across a single string using only a set of numbers.

Use the **Say It Three Times, Play It Three Times** method to first learn each scale, and the additional challenges to master them.

1 = Memorise   2 = First Playthrough   3 = 3x Forward   4 = 3x Backward   5 = All 6 Strings

The Major Scale
1 0 2 4 5 7 9 11 12   [1] [2] [3] [4] [5]

The Major Scale has the formula T T S T T T S

The Minor Scale
2 0 2 3 5 7 8 10 12   [1] [2] [3] [4] [5]

The Minor Scale has the formula T S T T S T T

The Major Pentatonic Scale
3 0 2 4 7 9 12   [1] [2] [3] [4] [5]

The Major Pentatonic Scale has the formula T T T.5 T T.5

The Minor Pentatonic Scale
4 0 3 5 7 10 12   [1] [2] [3] [4] [5]

The Minor Pentatonic Scale has the formula T.5 T T T.5 T

The Blues Scale
5 0 3 5 6 7 10 12   [1] [2] [3] [4] [5]

The Blues Scale has the formula T.5 T S S T.5 T

The Harmonic Minor Scale
6 0 2 3 5 7 8 11 12   [1] [2] [3] [4] [5]

The H/M Scale has the formula T S T T S T.5 S

The Whole Tone Scale
7 0 2 4 6 8 10 12   [1] [2] [3] [4] [5]

The Whole Tone Scale has the formula T T T T T T

The Double Harmonic Scale
8 0 1 4 5 7 8 11 12   [1] [2] [3] [4] [5]

The Double Harmonic Scale has the formula S T.5 S T S T.5 S

The Melodic Minor Scale
9 0 2 3 5 7 9 11 12   [1] [2] [3] [4] [5]

The Melodic Minor Scale has the formula T S T T T T S

The Diminished Scale
10 0 1 3 4 6 7 9 10 12   [1] [2] [3] [4] [5]

The Diminished Scale has the formula S T S T S T S T

Speed Tracker										
BPM	Ex 1	Ex 2	Ex 3	Ex 4	Ex 5	Ex 6	Ex 7	Ex 8	Ex 9	Ex 10
60										
80										
100										
120										

VERTICAL SCALES

When you play scales across a single string you will notice that there is a lot of lateral movement. Luckily, the layout of the guitar allows us to conveniently play scales across multiple strings. These two-note and three-note per-string scales make it easy to play a lot of notes without having to move your hands all over the neck. Use the 5 challenges below to learn and practice your vertical scales.

1 = 3x Each String.   2 = Put It Together   3 = 3x Up   4 = 3x Down   5 = 3x Up & Down

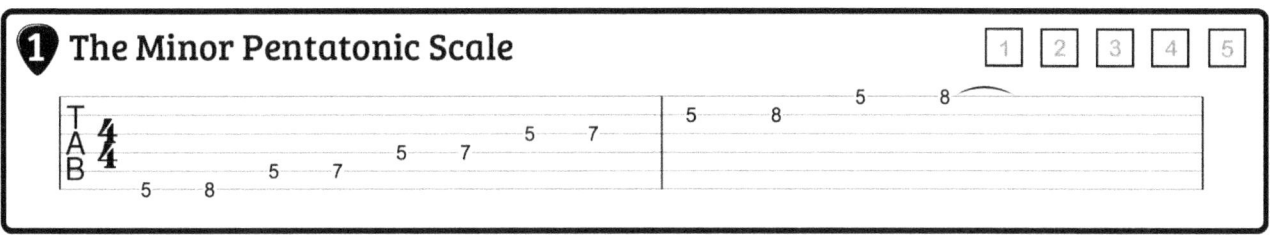

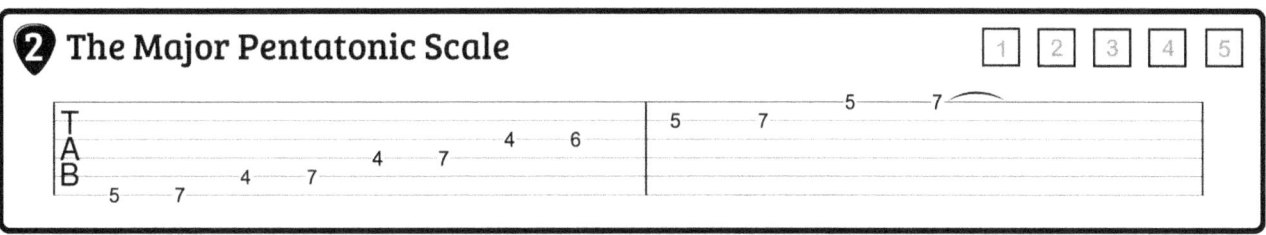

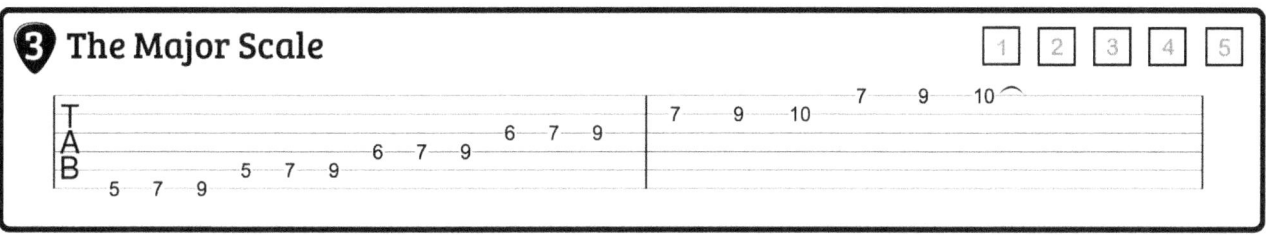

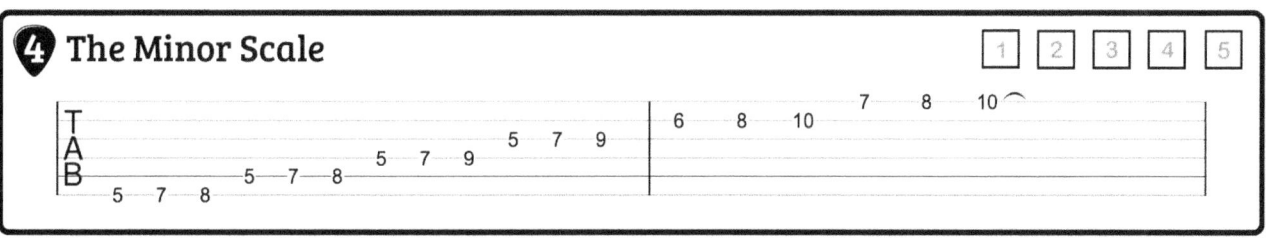

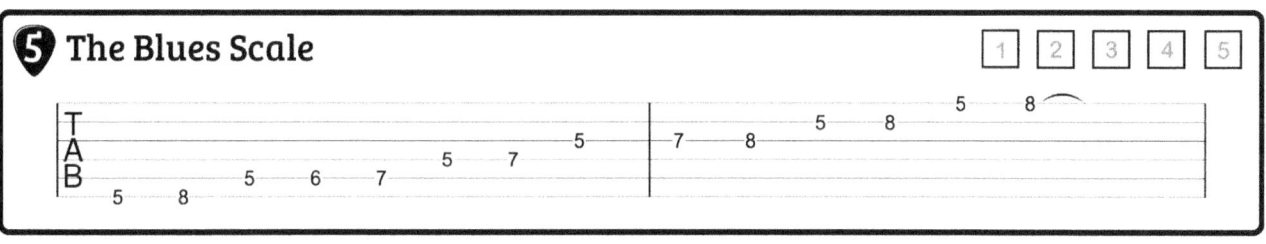

Speed Tracker										
BPM	60	70	80	90	100	120	130	140	150	160
Minor Pentatonic										
Major Pentatonic										
Major										
Minor										
Blues										

© Melbourne Guitar Academy
www.MelbourneGuitarAcademy.com

Part 2

The Level-Up System

Did you know that a whopping 90% of people who begin learning how to play the guitar end up quitting within the first 12 months?

It's a staggering statistic and a clear sign that something is wrong with the traditional way most people learn guitar. While education in most other fields has evolved over the past few decades, music lessons often stick to centuries-old methods that are out of touch with the needs of today's learners.

But don't worry, we've come up with a solution! We've developed a completely fresh approach to learning the guitar that delivers much better results. Instead of repeating the same old methods and expecting different results (we all know that's the definition of insanity), our approach is innovative, efficient, and customized to meet the needs of modern learners.

Say goodbye to the overwhelm and frustration that often leads to early quitting, and get ready to thrive on your guitar journey!

Lesson 20 - The Level Up System

When first starting to learn the guitar, most of us begin by trying to play the same chords we hear our favourite musicians use in their songs.

The problem with this approach is that it takes most people 6-12 months just to learn and remember these "*basic*" chord shapes, and longer still to develop the ability to smoothly switch between these chords while strumming.

As beginners, we get frustrated because we expect to be as good as our favourite artists right from the beginning. We compare ourselves to them, even though they've been playing for years while we've only just begun our guitar journey a few weeks or a few months earlier. This can make us doubt ourselves and lead to us wanting to quit playing the guitar altogether. But it's not a fair comparison...

Think of it like this: Imagine you started playing basketball just three weeks ago. You wouldn't expect to be as good as Michael Jordan or LeBron James right? So, why put that kind of pressure on yourself when you're learning the guitar?

Here's the important thing to remember: Learning guitar takes time, and its usually 2-3 years before most people become truly comfortable with playing guitar to even a basic level. So, embrace the learning process, allow yourself to make mistakes and don't worry about sounding like a beginner during this time.

Keep in mind that it's all part of the learning journey. With dedication and patience, you'll improve and achieve your goals!

Most People Take The Wrong Approach To Learning Chords

I believe that the traditional approach to learning chords is incorrect and won't work for 90% of people!

Think of it this way: Suppose I were your trainer at the gym, and I tried to get you to bench press a 100kg (220lb) weight on your very first day.

There would be a 99.9% chance that you wouldn't be able to do it. No matter how hard you tried or how many attempts you took, you would only end up fatigued and frustrated by your repeated failures.

The Level-Up System

It's clear that attempting to lift weights that are too heavy for us is a bad idea within the context of a gym exercise. Yet, when it comes to learning guitar, we often dive right into the deep end and try to play chords that are way beyond our level, only to get frustrated when we can't do them.

Trying to learn *Bar Chords*, is like attempting to lift 100kg weights without working our way up to it. It's just not going to happen without several weeks or even months of practice.

Even *Standard Open Chords*, which are found in every contemporary beginner guitar book are equivalent to lifting 80kg weights and require a lot of effort to work up to.

This unrealistic approach to learning chords results in many people quitting guitar prematurely because they lack the patience or discipline to stick with it for the 6-12 months it takes for the complex movements required to play chords and transition between them smoothly (while strumming) become part of your muscle memory.

But fear not, there is a better way, and I'm here to teach it to you!

Introducing The Level-Up System

If we were in a gym and I was training you to do a 100kg (220lb) bench press, here is the process I would take:

- I would introduce you to the exercise with a broomstick and make sure you were doing everything correctly with a 0% chance of failure or hurting yourself.
- Once you can perform the exercise correctly with no weight, I would upgrade you to a light metal bar of 5-10kg.
- Once you could perform the bench press correctly to a specific number of reps I would increase the difficulty by giving you a 20kg Olympic bar.
- Over the next few weeks and months, we would gradually add additional weight plates and progressively increase the weight you were lifting and the number of reps you performed until you reached your goal of benching 100kg.

It might take us months or even years to get there, but as long as we consistently work towards our goal and put in the work required, we will eventually get there.

The Level-Up System

Applying This Approach To Guitar

It's essential to let go of any preconceived ideas about the "*right way*" to learn guitar or what your playing should sound like when you're just starting out.

Here's a fact: 90% of people who begin learning how to play the guitar end up quitting within the first 12 months. I can guarantee you that if you follow the same traditional path as everyone else, you'll likely end up with the same outcome - quitting in your first year!

So instead, we're going to break down guitar playing into different levels and redefine what success means for a beginner guitarist. We'll gradually tackle more challenging levels as we gain experience and improve our finger control and coordination.

Here's how this leveled approach to learning guitar works:

- Level 1 - Single Note Bass Lines
- Level 2 - Power Chords
- Level 3 - One Finger Triads
- Level 4 - Simplified Open Chords
- Level 5 - Standard Open Chords (where many people struggle and give up)
- Level 6 - Bar Chords (I don't recommend for beginners)

Instead of starting at Level 5 or 6 with Open or Bar Chords like most people do and wondering why the guitar is so hard, we'll instead begin at Level 1 and play along to a complete song using just one finger on one string. This is known as playing the **Bassline** and is something you will pick up very quickly.

Once we can comfortably play the bassline, we move on to Level 2 where we level up to **Power Chords**. These chords are more challenging but will make the piece sound a lot fuller and will be a step closer to what you hear on the recording.

As we progress, the next step is Level 3 where we use movable **One Finger Triads**.

Each time we level up, our playing sounds more and more like the original recording until we work our way up to playing using the same chords as we hear on the recording.

The Level-Up System For Chords

Climbing The Ladder

Until now, we've mainly discussed what our fretting hand does when it comes to playing different levels of chords on the guitar.

Guitar playing can be challenging because we must coordinate two hands at the same time, each performing distinct movements simultaneously.

Imagine trying to switch between unfamiliar chord shapes while also strumming a complex rhythm pattern with your other hand. It's like attempting to drive a manual car for the first time - overwhelmingly complicated!

Just as our Fretting Hand has different levels for chords, our Picking Hand also progresses through levels for strumming and picking patterns. Here's a basic overview:

- Level 1 - One pick/strum per bar
- Level 2 - Four picks/strums per bar
- Level 3 - A simplified picking/strumming pattern
- Level 4 - The written picking/strumming pattern
- Level 5 - A more complex picking/strumming pattern

I use the ladder analogy for the **Level-Up System** because a ladder has two sides, reflecting the two distinct roles our hands have when we play the guitar.

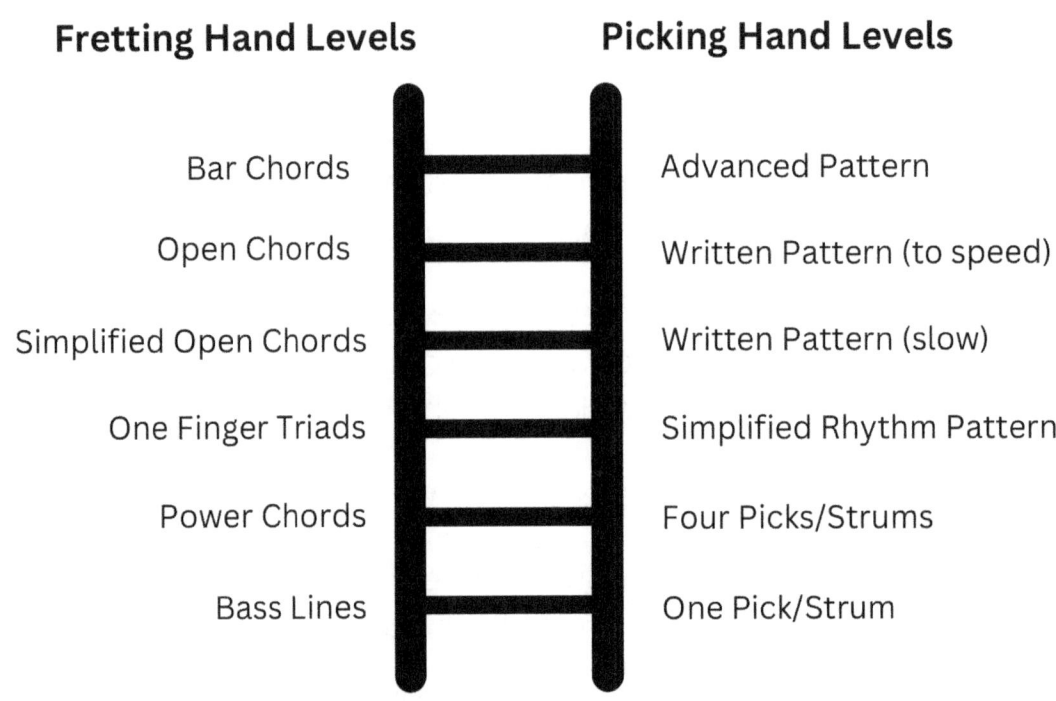

How To Play Along To Any Song

If you know the names of the notes on the 6th string then you have everything you need to play along with your favourite songs.

All you have to do is play the root note of each chord in the progression in time with the music. This is called "*playing the bassline*" and it's what bass players do within a band or orchestra. Playing the bassline is Level 1 in the Level-Up System.

Playing the bassline is a fantastic way to start building your musicianship skills and allows you to play along with most songs right away.

How To Play The Bassline

To play a bassline for any song, find the notes on the 6th string that match the name of the chords in the progression. Let it ring out for the duration of the bar. Let's take an example using the chord progression from *Knocking On Heaven's Door*.

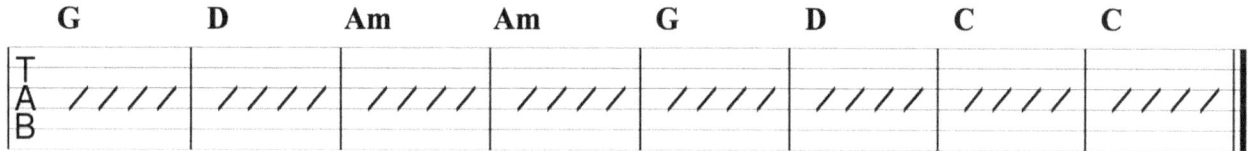

In *Knocking On Heaven's Door*, the chords are G, D, Am, Am, then G, D, C, C. To play along with the song, find the frets where the notes G, D, A, and C are located on the 6th string. Use the diagram of the notes on String 6 below to help you:

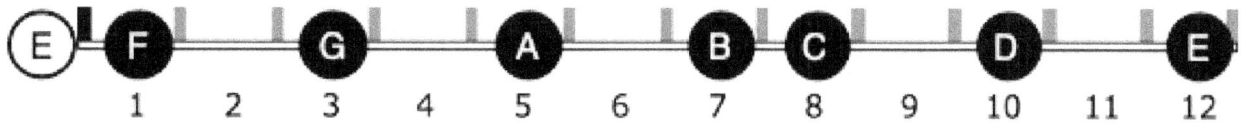

So, to play the song's bassline, all you need to do is play the frets in this order: 3, 10, 5, 5, then 3, 10, 8, 8 in time with the music. It's incredibly easy! Here are the tabs for reference:

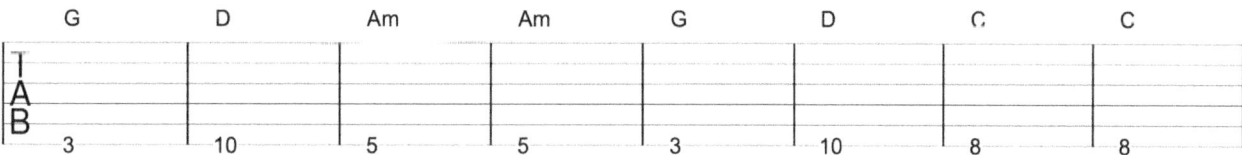

Level 2 - Power Chords

Power Chords are a special type of chord shape that can be used in place of any Major or Minor chord.

Instead of needing to learn and memorize more than a dozen different chord shapes and having to work on changing between them smoothly, you can just learn the Power Chord shape and move it around the guitar neck to play any chord. Here are the Power Chord shapes:

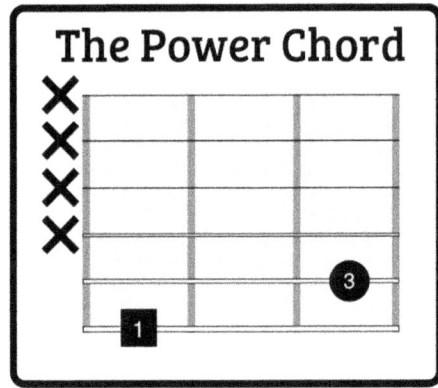
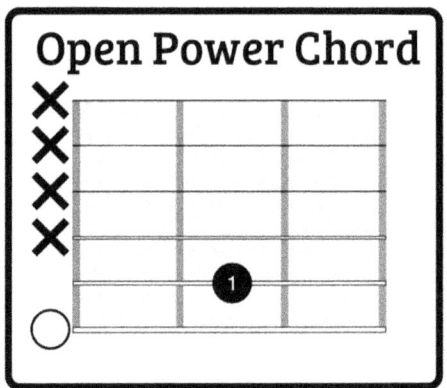

Power Chords are named after the note they are played from.

For example, to play the F Power Chord (written as F5), place your first finger on the F note at fret 1 on the 6th string and your third finger on the 3rd fret of the 5th string. **Your third finger is always two frets higher on the string above where your first finger is**. The diagram below shows the notes along strings 5 & 6 to help you locate where to play each chord:

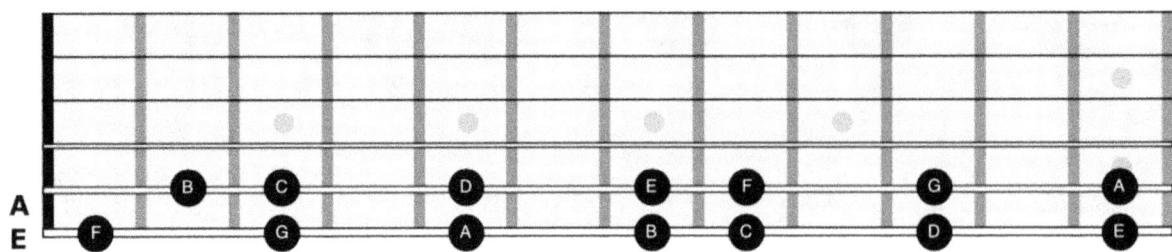

Here is Knocking On Heaven's Door using Power Chords:

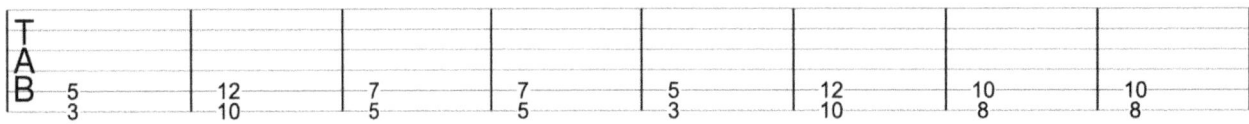

Level 3 - One Finger Triads

A Triad is the smallest form of a chord that contains just three notes. If you're learning how to play chords on a piano, you start by learning triads.

However, on the guitar, we usually jump straight into using 5 and 6 string open chords, which can be quite challenging. Triads are often introduced much later in the learning process.

Level 3 in our Level-Up System introduces two triad shapes: the Minor Triad shape and the Major Triad shape. Here's the best part, you can play these two shapes with just one finger!

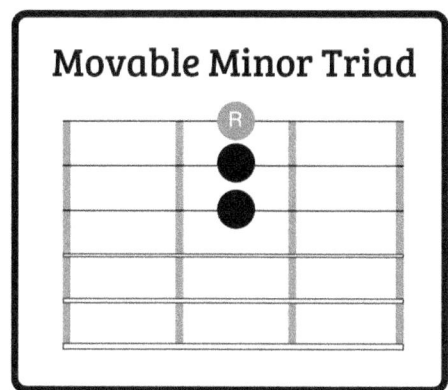
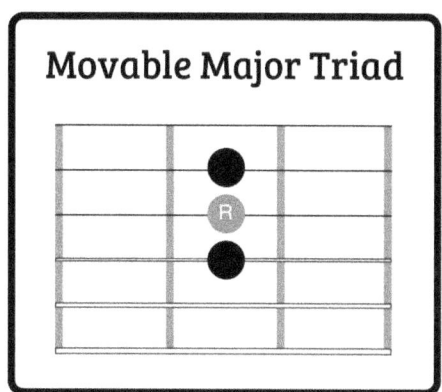

You can play any Minor Chord using the *Movable Minor Triad Shape* on the first three strings. Simply place your first finger across the first three strings, making sure that it lines up with the fret at which the root note is found, then strum. For example, if you want to play a G Minor Chord, use the shape at fret 3. (cover fret 3 on strings 1-3)

The *Movable Major Triad* works the same way, but you'll use the shape on strings 2-4 instead. Position your finger over the root note found on string 3 and strum. For instance, if you want to play a D chord, use the shape at fret 7 and strum strings 2, 3, and 4. The notes along strings 1 and 3 are provided below as a reference (note that the open position works too).

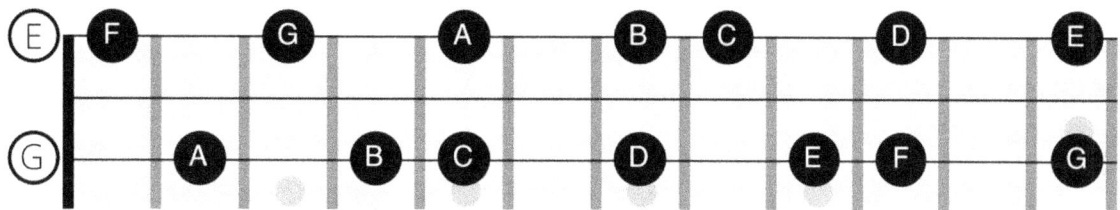

Here is Knocking On Heaven's Door using One Finger Movable Triads

```
      G         D         Am        Am        G         D         C         C
                          5         5
                          5         5
T     0         7         5         5         0         7         5         5
A  4  0         7         5         5         0         7         5         5
B  4  0         7                             0         7         5         5
```

Levelled Chord Progressions

A **Chord Progression** is when you play two or more chords one after the other. Most songs are simply chord progressions with singing over the top of them.

A chord progression will generally be notated as follows:

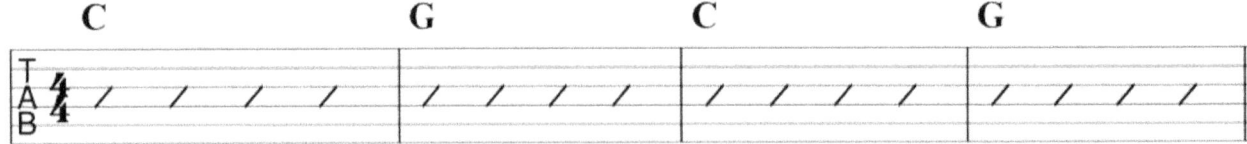

You can see that you need to play a C chord in the first bar, and a G chord in the second bar, another C chord in the 3rd bar and a G chord in the fourth bar.

The dashes are used to signal strums. If you see / / / / you need to strum four times on each chord before changing to the new chord.

How To Play Chord Progressions

- Put your fingers in the right place for the C chord.
- Strum four times.
- Switch your fingers to the right place for the G chord.
- Strum four times.
- Repeat this over and over for 20 repetitions, or two minutes, whichever comes first.

How To Play Chord Progressions Using The Level-Up System

As stated earlier, it's going to take months to get comfortable with traditional chord changes. Instead of making your life difficult, we'll instead focus on playing chord progressions in three levels:

Fretting Hand

- Level 1 - Bass Lines
- Level 2 - Power Chords
- Level 3 - One Finger Triads

Picking Hand

- Level 1 - One Pick/Strum
- Level 2 - Four Picks/Strums
- Level 3 - Simple Pattern

Once you get comfortable with these three levels you can explore additional chords found in your Guitar Workbook 1.

Levelled Chord Progressions

Over the next few pages, we're going to take you through 10 of the most common chord progressions used in contemporary guitar music and pop songs.

Each progression will be presented in the key of G Major with three levels for you to work through for each hand.

The sooner you memorise your chord shapes and develop the ability to change between them smoothly, the sooner you can play real songs. These chord progressions will prepare you for playing your favourite tunes.

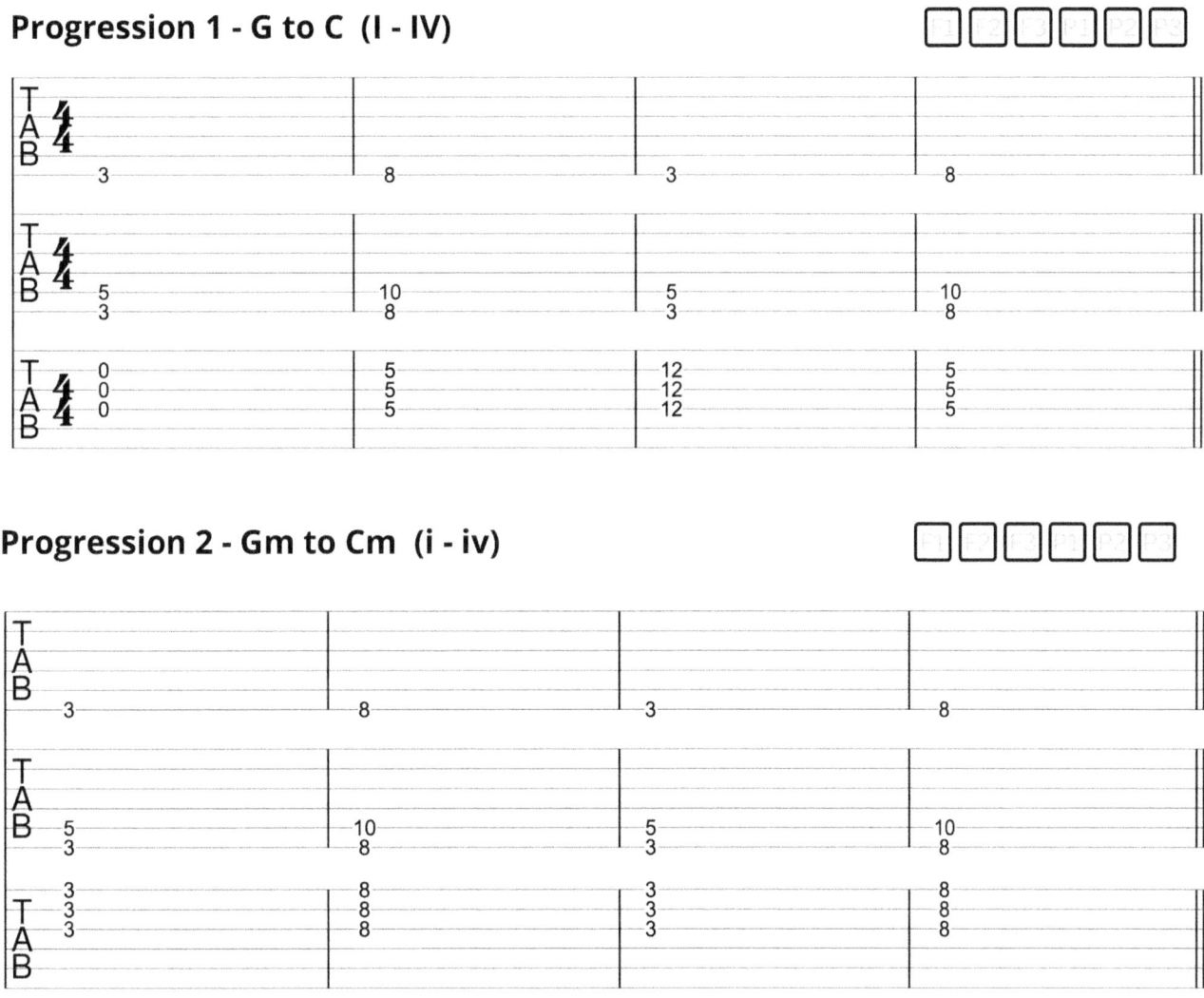

Tip: Play the progression 3x in a row without a mistake at level 1 before moving on to the next level. You can use the checkboxes to keep track of which level you are up to with each hand.

Tip: The G and Em chords can be played at fret 0 or fret 12. You can use just 0's, just 12's or a combination of both when playing progressions that use these chords. We recommend using the option with less movement.

Levelled Chord Progressions

Progression 3 - G to D (I - V)

```
T|--------------------|--------------------|--------------------|--------------------||
A|--------------------|--------------------|--------------------|--------------------||
B|--3-----------------|--10----------------|--3-----------------|--10----------------||

T|--------------------|--------------------|--------------------|--------------------||
A|--5-----------------|--12----------------|--5-----------------|--12----------------||
B|--3-----------------|--10----------------|--3-----------------|--10----------------||

T|--0-----------------|--7-----------------|--12----------------|--7-----------------||
A|--0-----------------|--7-----------------|--12----------------|--7-----------------||
B|--0-----------------|--7-----------------|--12----------------|--7-----------------||
```

Progression 4 - Gm to Dm (i - v)

```
T|--------------------|--------------------|--------------------|--------------------||
A|--------------------|--------------------|--------------------|--------------------||
B|--3-----------------|--10----------------|--3-----------------|--10----------------||

T|--------------------|--------------------|--------------------|--------------------||
A|--5-----------------|--12----------------|--5-----------------|--12----------------||
B|--3-----------------|--10----------------|--3-----------------|--10----------------||

T|--3-----------------|--7-----------------|--3-----------------|--7-----------------||
A|--3-----------------|--7-----------------|--3-----------------|--7-----------------||
B|--3-----------------|--7-----------------|--3-----------------|--7-----------------||
```

Progression 5 - G to C to D to G (I - IV - V - I)

```
T|--------------------|--------------------|--------------------|--------------------||
A|--------------------|--------------------|--------------------|--------------------||
B|--3-----------------|--8-----------------|--10----------------|--3-----------------||

T|--------------------|--------------------|--------------------|--------------------||
A|--5-----------------|--10----------------|--12----------------|--5-----------------||
B|--3-----------------|--8-----------------|--10----------------|--3-----------------||

T|--0-----------------|--5-----------------|--7-----------------|--12----------------||
A|--0-----------------|--5-----------------|--7-----------------|--12----------------||
B|--0-----------------|--5-----------------|--7-----------------|--12----------------||
```

Levelled Chord Progressions

Progression 6 - Gm to Cm to D to Gm (i - iv - V - i)

```
T|--------------|--------------|--------------|--------------||
A|--------------|--------------|--------------|--------------||
B|--3-----------|--8-----------|--10----------|--3-----------||

T|--5-----------|--10----------|--12----------|--5-----------||
A|--3-----------|--8-----------|--10----------|--3-----------||
B|--------------|--------------|--------------|--------------||

T|--3-----------|--8-----------|--------------|--3-----------||
A|--3-----------|--8-----------|--7-----------|--3-----------||
B|--3-----------|--8-----------|--7-----------|--3-----------||
                                 --7-----------
```

Progression 7 - G to C to D to C (I - IV - V - IV)

```
T|--------------|--------------|--------------|--------------||
A|--------------|--------------|--------------|--------------||
B|--3-----------|--8-----------|--10----------|--8-----------||

T|--5-----------|--10----------|--12----------|--10----------||
A|--3-----------|--8-----------|--10----------|--8-----------||
B|--------------|--------------|--------------|--------------||

T|--0-----------|--5-----------|--7-----------|--5-----------||
A|--0-----------|--5-----------|--7-----------|--5-----------||
B|--0-----------|--5-----------|--7-----------|--5-----------||
```

Progression 8 - G to C to Em to D to G (I - IV - vi - V)

```
T|--------------|--------------|--------------|--------------||
A|--------------|--------------|--------------|--------------||
B|--3-----------|--10----------|--0-----------|--8-----------||

T|--5-----------|--12----------|--2-----------|--10----------||
A|--3-----------|--10----------|--0-----------|--8-----------||
B|--------------|--------------|--------------|--------------||

T|--0-----------|--7-----------|--0-----------|--5-----------||
A|--0-----------|--7-----------|--0-----------|--5-----------||
B|--0-----------|--7-----------|--0-----------|--5-----------||
```

Levelled Chord Progressions

Progression 9 - G to Em to C to D (I - vi - IV - V)

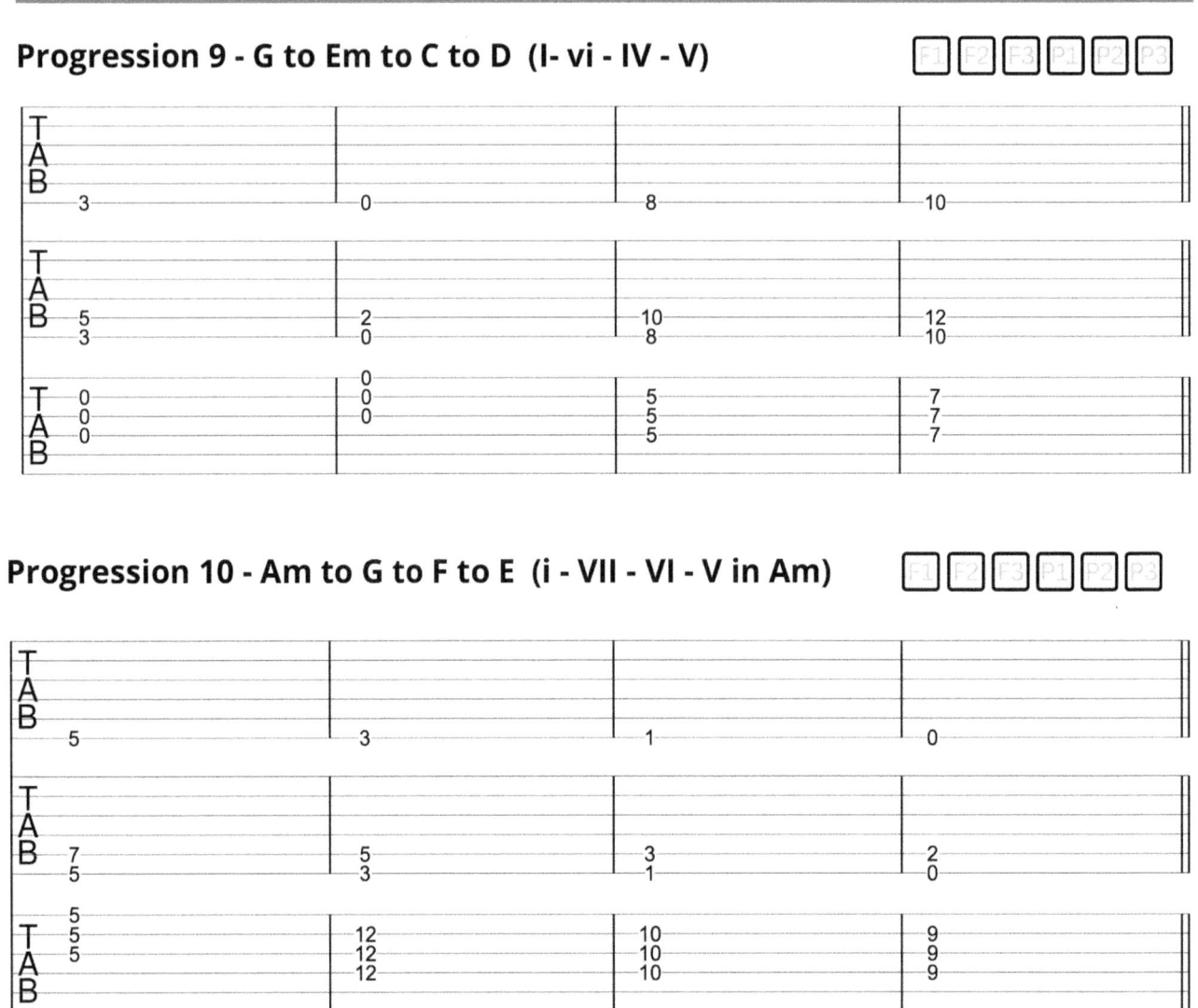

Progression 10 - Am to G to F to E (i - VII - VI - V in Am)

Taking It To The Next Level

Once you start getting the hang of the One Finger Triads you can begin exploring higher-level chords found in your Guitar Workbook 1

- Additional Chords can be found from page 10 onwards
- Additional Chord Progressions can be found from pg 21 onwards
- Additional Strumming Patterns can be found on pages 27 onwards

You do not need to complete this entire book before you start these additional levels. You can move onto a new level of chords as soon as changing between your current chords becomes seamless.

Bonus Lesson - The Four Chord Progression

There is a very special chord progression known as the *Four Chord Progression* that is used in thousands and thousands of well-known songs!

It used the chords C, G, Am & F.

We've given you an overview of how to play the *Four Chord Progression* in seven levels all the way from a simple Bassline to the challenging Barre Chords.

The Four Chord Progression - C G Am F

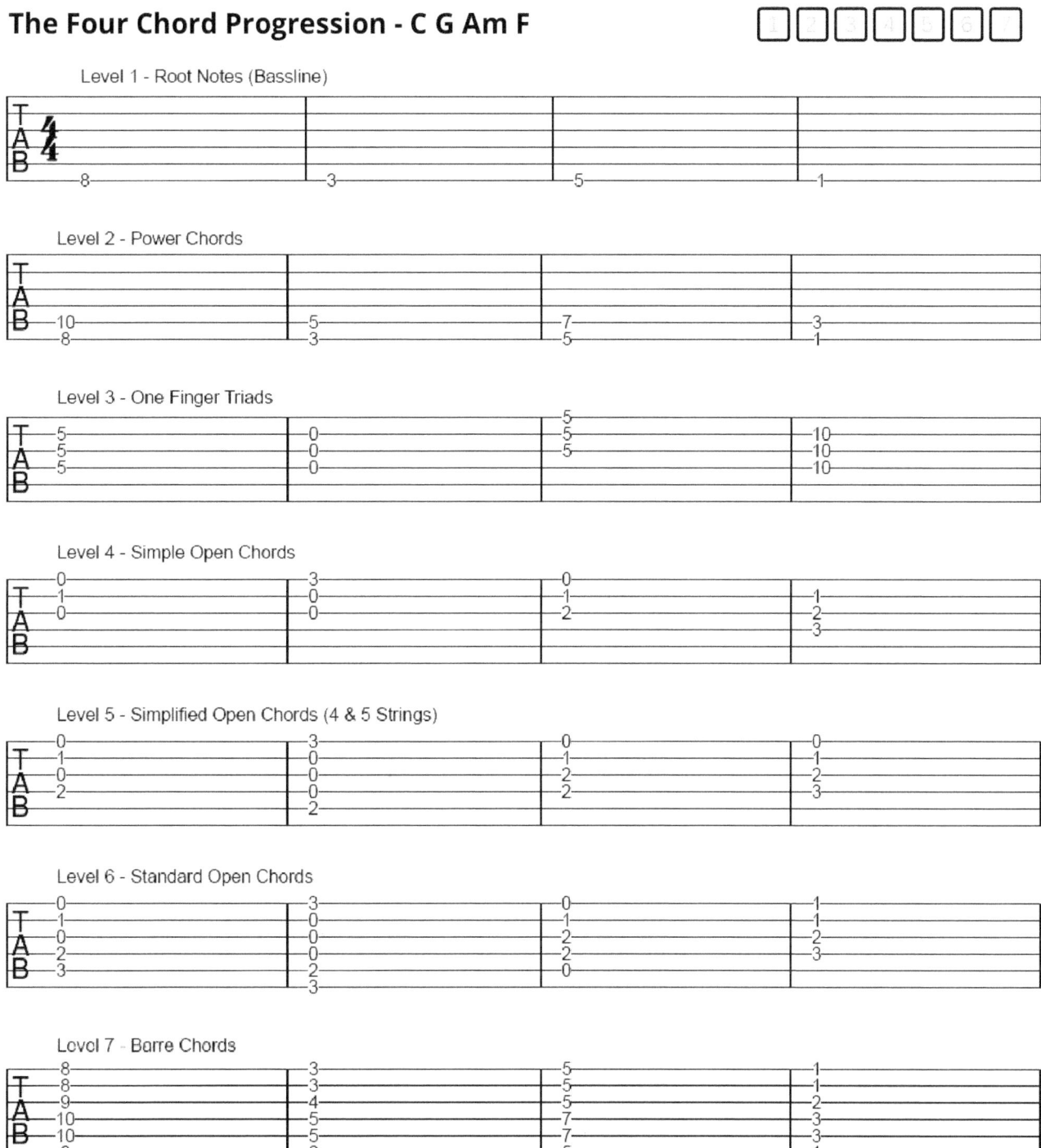

Strumming Pattern Drills

A strumming pattern is a rhythm that we apply to a chord progression to make it sound more interesting. It's essential that you build up a repertoire of a dozen or so go-to strumming patterns that you can use when playing songs.

Use the 5 steps below to learn and memorise any Strumming Pattern:

1 = Clap & Count   2 = Clap & Say Direction   3 = 5x Muted   4 = 5x Single Chord   5 = 5x Progression

o = 4 counts   𝄐 = 2 counts   ♩ = 1 counts   ♫ = ½ + ½ count

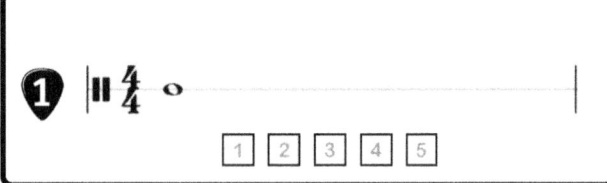 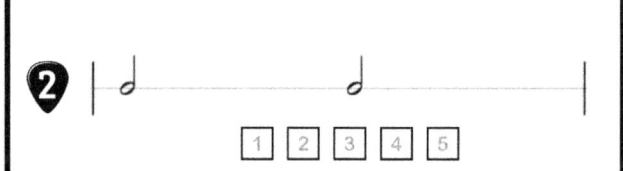
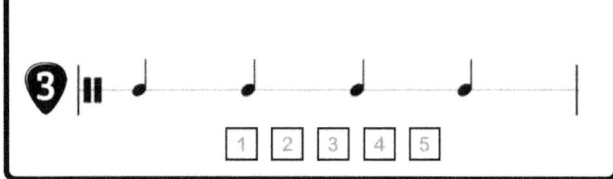 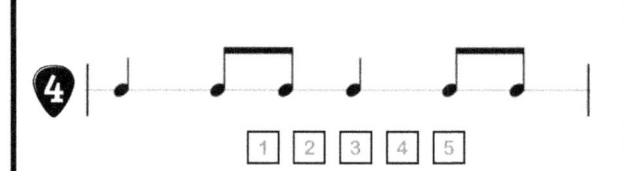
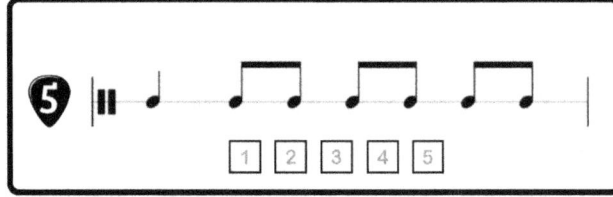 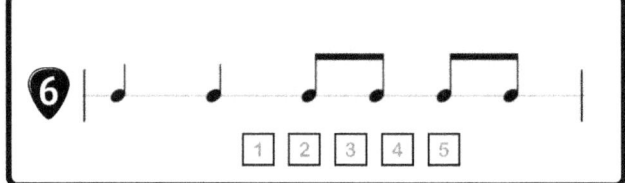
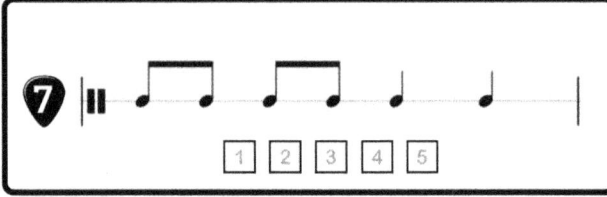 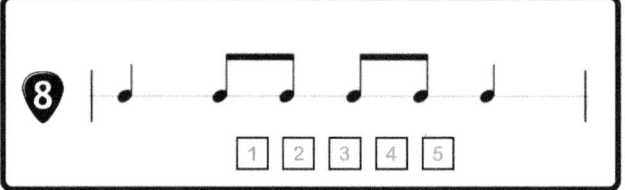

Speed Tracker								
BPM	Ex 1	Ex 2	Ex 3	Ex 4	Ex 5	Ex 6	Ex 7	Ex 8
60								
80								
100								
120								

Strumming Pattern Drills 2

In addition to using basic rhythms, we can also use rests to create interesting rhythms and strumming patterns. A rest is where you don't play any sounds and mute any strings ringing out for a set duration.

Below are 8 Strumming Patterns that use Rests:

1 = Clap & Count 2 = Clap & Say Direction 3 = 5x Muted 4 = 5x Single Chord 5 = 5x Progression

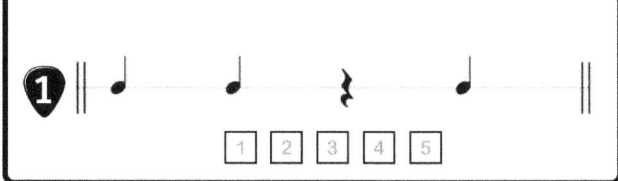
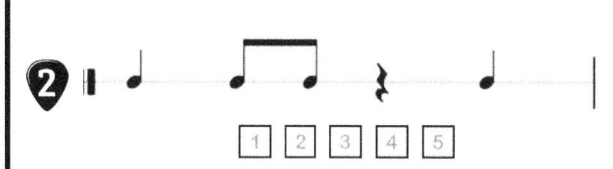
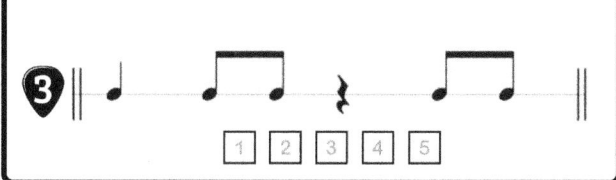
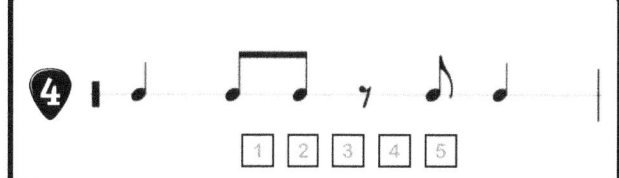
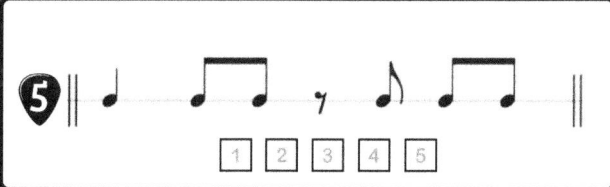
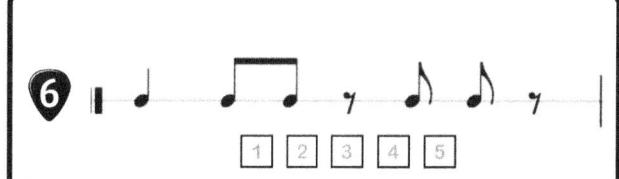
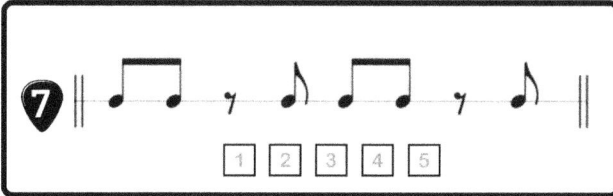
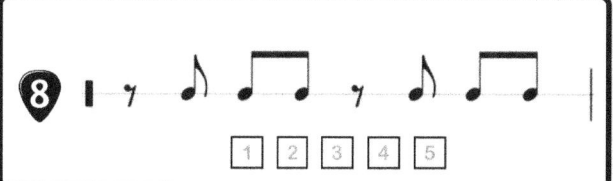

Speed Tracker								
BPM	Ex 1	Ex 2	Ex 3	Ex 4	Ex 5	Ex 6	Ex 7	Ex 8
60								
80								
100								
120								

Guitar Practice Log

Name: _____   Month: _____

Date of Day 1 = _____   Date of Day 30/31 = _____

Practice Area	1	2	3	4	5	6	7	8	9	10	11	12	13	14	15	16	17	18	19	20	21	22	23	24	25	26	27	28	29	30	31
Study Pieces																															
Warmups																															
Scales																															
Melodies																															
Riffs																															
Chord Memorisation																															
Chord Progressions																															
Strumming Patterns																															
Rhythms																															
Note Memorisation																															
Songs & Repertoire																															

How To Use

Easy: Cross off the box that matches each practice item you worked on for that day.

Advanced: Write the number of minutes you practiced each item for in the corresponding box.

- 1 complete — 3 Days In A Row
- 2 complete — 10 Days In A Row
- 3 complete — 15 Days In A Row
- 4 complete — Practice On 20 Or More Days
- 5 complete — Every Day Of The Month — Complete Special Prize!

© Melbourne Guitar Academy
Adult Guitar Method Book
www.MelbourneGuitarAcademy.com

www.ingramcontent.com/pod-product-compliance
Lightning Source LLC
Chambersburg PA
CBHW060357010526
44109CB00051B/2504